CW01497320

WILD SHETLAND

THROUGH THE SEASONS

WILD SHETLAND
THROUGH THE SEASONS

Brydon Thomason

The Shetland Times Ltd
Lerwick
2023

WILD SHETLAND

THROUGH THE SEASONS

ISBN 978-1-910997-56-7

A catalogue record for this book is available from the British Library.

Printed and published by
The Shetland Times Ltd.,
Gremista, Lerwick,
Shetland ZE1 0PX.

Tae mam and dad,
it's aa thanks tae you.

CONTENTS

FOREWORD

This is an absolute corker of a book. As a foreword, that's all you really need to know, but I will qualify exactly why I've used this phrase.

From the first page to the last, Brydon Thomason's stunning photographs jump out at you. Each and every one is a stunner, but not only is Brydon an excellent photographer, he is also an ethical one, and a superb all-round naturalist.

I first met him whilst filming on Shetland for the BBC's *Springwatch* series a decade ago. He advised us on where and how to film much of the archipelago's incredible wildlife, but every time we ventured out, he drummed into us that the welfare of the wildlife has to come first. On visits to several otter locations, thanks to his knowledge and fieldcraft, we were able to get the required footage without causing any disturbance whatsoever.

His passion, his vast photographic abilities and his deep Shetland roots ooze from every page. The mix of local dialect and Norse names are sprinkled throughout the book as he takes us through the four seasons in the far north. As well as looking at some of the islands' specialities, such as Red-necked Phalarope, Orca and Whimbrel, we also get insights into the seasonal lives of species such as the Wren, Ringed Plover and Grey Seal. Shetland's plants and invertebrates also feature, again lavishly illustrated with Brydon's beautiful photographs.

Brydon also draws attention to the struggles many species face, and the need for us to make fundamental changes if we are to ensure their survival and that of our environment.

During my several visits to Shetland, I've always felt there was one thing missing. A book showcasing the islands' wildlife, with short snippets of information on each species. This handsome tome fills that void. Whether you are planning a future visit to this unique place, looking for a memento to take away or merely a collector of beautiful books, this is the one for you.

Buy it, enjoy it, read it from cover to cover, then visit this special group of islands.

Iolo Williams
Television naturalist and presenter.

As a young lad Brydon Thomason was greatly inspired by Bobby Tulloch, Shetland's nature tourism pioneer and the RSPB's officer in the isles. It was 'Bobby the Birdman' who found the Snowy Owls breeding on Fetlar in 1967 – before Brydon was born. But happily for Brydon, some 'Snowies' remained on the island throughout his childhood, although sadly no longer breeding.

Brydon was fascinated to hear from both Bobby and me about our experiences of the nesting owls. Bobby set up a hide to enable me to make a film for the RSPB. For him, in those pre-ferry days, quite a logistical challenge; he had to organise teams to mount 24-hour guards on the nest – hundreds of visitors came, and as for the media... My greatest moment was catching sight of the first newly-hatched Snowy Owl chick in Britain to ever hatch in the wild! And I was the first person to see it.

Years later, near that same old nest site, Brydon photographed a majestic male Snowy Owl perched on a post. The camera has captured the ghostly-white owl's expression of wide-eyed astonishment, no doubt the feeling was mutual.

Discussing this book with Brydon and sharing our own experiences with cameras, it is remarkable to see how photography has changed. I could tell Brydon about several of Shetland's first wildlife photographers I knew, who are no longer with us.

The best-known of these was surely JD Rattar. Although inhibited by the simple uncluttered cameras of an earlier era, he photographed birds and views of Shetland on large glass plates. In the late 1940s I often watched him hand-tinting the sepia prints he framed to sell in his Commercial Street shop.

About 1950 I recall Theo Kay filming Gannets diving in large numbers among sillicks that used to shoal in masses around Lerwick piers. He and his son Billy photographed our four seasons and gave shows in packed country halls in the years before the arrival of television in 1964. They used hides made by taxidermist Sammy Bruce, who 'obtained' his birds with a walking-stick gun, often carried inside his coat hooked into the armpit.

In 1948 customs officer Jack Peterson published his first book illustrating Shetland's seasons with their scenic views, flowers, birds, seals (but none of Brydon's favourite Otters!); people at work, fishing and crofting, etc. Several years after his death, a second book was published in 1985, portraying the isles during the rapidly-changing post-war years. His photos in black and white add a feeling of nostalgia now, of a long-gone Shetland way of life.

Enter the young Brydon Thomason from Fetlar, island of charming Red-necked Phalaropes. With his fieldcraft, modern vision and imagination, he has created such brilliant images. No more the dated static 'portrait' of a single bird. Instead, his birds and mammals are so often in action, in well-composed groups, or squabbling; there's Otters surfing, family groups at feeding time, quaint *contre-jour* Puffins and as for that stunning back-lit Gannet in flight!

Whether it is Brydon's shots of colourful skies or Bonxies in unseasonal snow, his timely images were made in all weathers. They not only convey his vivid awareness of our wonderful Shetland environment, but will cause others to appreciate what surrounds us even more.

Here is nature photography in an entirely new league. This book is a winner!

Dennis Coutts

Dennis is one of Shetland's most successful and best-known photographers, whose career spanned five decades, from 1950s till retirement in 1990s.

ACKNOWLEDGEMENTS

It would have been impossible to give this book the heart and soul I have without the help of others. With those who know me well there has been continuing repartee about the longevity of the project and, in fairness, that has not been misplaced as the project has been on and off the shelf over more years than I care to remember.

Giving thanks, I must begin with my family. To my wife, Vaila, for her love, support and encouragement that I am so lucky to have, and without which, none of what I do would be possible. And, to our amazing bairns, who might not even be aware of the help they have given. Our sons Casey (14), and Corey (12), and daughter Nula (7), are a greater inspiration to me than all of Shetland's species combined.

Before I acknowledge people for help that relates to this book, I must thank the naturalists who encouraged my interest in nature from childhood, as did my family, particularly my grandfather, Ollie Tait, and fellow islanders. Nick Dymond, the late Mike Peacock, Dennis Coutts and the late Bobby Tulloch undoubtedly set my course and, later, Pete Ellis, Mike Pennington, Paul Harvey and Roger Riddington were especially generous with their time.

I am very grateful to many authors and researchers and, where appropriate, some are credited within the captions. I am, however, particularly grateful to Steve Votier, Malcie Smith, Mark Bolton, Will Miles, Dave Hunt, Richard Sale, Rob Hughes and Andy Foote. Should any inaccuracies or misquotes be discovered, here or elsewhere, I accept full responsibility.

I have found many sources of information online and in books, but for the latter, I feel these titles particularly relevant to mention: *The Birds of Shetland* (Pennington, Osborn, Harvey, Riddington, Okill, Ellis and Heubeck); *A Naturalists Shetland* (Laughton Johnston); *Bobby Tulloch's Shetland* and *The Seabird's Cry* (Adam Nicolson).

For favours, gadgets borrowed, boat trips enjoyed, land permission and hide work logistics, I am eternally grateful to Robbie Brookes and Peter Hunter and the following people: Josh Jaggard; Dave Cooper; Richard Shucksmith; Kevin Kelly; Phil Harris (Shetland Seabird Tours); Darron and Rodney Smith (Mousa Boat); Dennis Johnson; Philip Niven; James Rogerson; Molly Michelin; Derek Jamieson; Christopher Ritch; Shaun Manson; Connel MacDonald; Andy Parkinson, Richard Bennet, Matt Bruce and the NatureScot Licensing team.

I also want to thank Peter Antoniou for his ongoing support over the many years that I have been fortunate to work as a brand ambassador with Swarovski Optik and also, more recently, Mark Hoskins of Benro UK. For writing retreats I am grateful to Sarah and David Kerr, Martha and Malcie Smith, Kenny and Mai Gear, and Tom Morton and Susan Bowie.

I have quoted Shetland dialect poetry and songs, which I hope add an extra layer of our cultural heritage. These are all credited to the authors, past and present, but I also want to thank Chloe Tallack, Laurie Goodlad and Andrea Manson for their suggested reading.

For the Foreword, I am forever thankful to Iolo Williams. Knowing him and his love of the islands, it feels particularly special for him to put his words and name to this book. Having Dennis Coutts also share his thoughts and memories feels like the ultimate authentication as there is unlikely to be a Shetland photographer better known throughout the isles. I am also so very grateful for the cover quotes from Ann Cleeves, Kate Humble and Patrick Barkham.

I want to say a massive thank you to Sophie Whitehead for my profile photo and Ingrid Sutherland for my hand-knitted Shetland ganzie, and also to John Coutts for his photo of Dennis.

Last, but absolutely by no means least, I owe so much to Jon Dunn and Mike Pennington for their edits and helpful suggestions on the text as it evolved.

INTRODUCTION

About this book

The Shetland Islands are a special place. Since the earliest settlers over 6,000 years ago, they have meant many things to many people. Chances are, by picking up this book you too have a connection to the isles – be it family, friends, a distant ancestry, or simply a love of our unique cultural and natural heritage. You may be like me, with the island way of life running through your veins, and Shetland is all of these things to you.

My aim with this book is to celebrate Shetland's wildlife through the changing seasons. To Shetlanders, traditionally living off the land long before the creation of a compass let alone modern day devices, using wildlife as seasonal indicators has always been a thread running through the fabric of everyday life. From the very first stirrings of spring through to the wildest winter storms, these connections with our local environment are part of what makes us who we are. They are the foundations of my love of the islands, and the inspiration for this book.

It may seem a strange confession from an author, but I do not see myself as much of a writer. Words have never come easily to me - it is artistically, particularly through the lens, that I feel I can best bring the seasons and the species in them to life. Though a coffee table picture-book would look nice, these subjects deserve so much more than photographs alone, regardless of the blood, sweat and tears expended to collate them. They are therefore accompanied with informative text that puts our most iconic wildlife into seasonal context, and blends historic observations with contemporary insight.

Through a combination of research along with my own passion, experiences and memories, I hope I've found a relatable tone in my writing style. This approach has also helped me explore the sense of identity and belonging we have as Shetlanders, whether we are born and raised here, or have taken the big decision to make the islands our home. Nonetheless, I firmly believe that it is the wildlife that's so special and important to share, not solely my perspective of it.

Though I have written this book to offer a lightsome overview of Shetland's seasonal wildlife, there is sadly a narrative of decline associated with many species. Whether we look at the natural world from a global or a local perspective, the negative effects of the pressures we have imposed on the natural world are unavoidable, and tangible in our everyday life. We witness them first-hand, and on our screens. We cannot, and should not, shy away from their reality.

As such, in these pages I highlight some of the main issues, but mainly try to find a balance to enjoy and appreciate the beauty and character of some truly magnificent creatures. We cannot afford to always view our natural world through rose-tinted glasses, but it is certainly good for the soul to put them on once in a while.

>>

The Shetland Islands

Located almost 161km from mainland Scotland, bordered by the Atlantic Ocean to the west and the North Sea to the east, the Shetland Islands are Britain's most northerly outpost. With the Faroe Islands nearly 290km to the west and the Norwegian coast some 225km east, the islands are truly remote.

Lying at 60°N the islands are on the same latitude as the southern tip of Greenland, and are closer to the Arctic Circle than they are to London. This geographic position helps provide context to the northern flavour of our flora and fauna, and gives rise to the islands' classification as Britain's only subarctic archipelago.

Shetland (please, never 'the Shetlands'), comprises over 100 islands, of which only 16 are inhabited by the total population of around 23,000 people. Shetland has a remarkable 2,731km of coastline yet a combined surface area of just 1,466 km^2. The islands have a relatively small landmass, yet they consist of a rich diversity of habitats laid over a complex geology. Although the islands lie in the face of unforgiving Atlantic low-pressure weather systems, and are dominated by the combined power of wind and wave, Shetland and its surrounding northern seas benefit from a relatively temperate oceanic climate generated by the Gulf Stream.

The weather and the seasons

Many aspects of our island life differ from the rest of Britain. There is however one that we share – our obsession with the weather. A recent study by social anthropologist Kate Fox found that the British are so influenced by our thoughts on the elements that, even when we are not out in them, at least one third of the country is either currently, recently, or about to talk about the weather!

If that's true in Britain as a whole, it's even more the case in Shetland. We have many sayings about the weather here, most of which reflect the relentless wind, driving rain, or the lack of sunshine! Not expecting too much of the weather is in our very heritage, and is an attitude you need to adopt if you move here.

Shetland's seasons merge slowly with one another, with each carrying with it signs of the last whilst offering just enough to suggest the coming of the next. It would be easy, and perhaps not entirely unjustified, to summarise that winters are long, wet and very windy, with summers short, cool and grey – ten months of winter followed by two of summer being a phrase often used here in jest.

This isn't entirely fair though, as we have many beautiful spells of weather, be they bright and breezy or calm and crisp, last a week or just one all too brief day. However, such is the power of these islands and the resilience of islanders who call them home, the love runs much deeper than blue skies and flaming sunsets.

SPRING

Shetland winters are long, and spring is slow to arrive. The powerful grip of strong winds, big seas and grey skies takes an eternity to ease. From late January onwards, the promise of fairer weather and the species that will return stirs hope and optimism for the months that lie ahead.

Though the months of January and February are often dominated by wild weather, it takes just a glimpse of the low winter sun, or a calm day *atween da wadders*, and we hear our smallest bird speak up for spring.

Owing to their tiny size, the dialect name I have always used for our resilient peerie songster is *broon button*. As with many familiar species here, their other local name derives from our Viking heritage – *sisti moos*, meaning 'mouse kin'.

There are six subspecies of Wren found in the British Isles, two of which are endemic to Shetland. Of these, *zetlandicus* is found throughout all of Shetland, while Fair Isle has the rarest subspecies of them all, *fridariensis*, comprising a population of barely 50 pairs of birds. Like the two endemic island subspecies found on St Kilda and the Western Isles, our Wrens are hardy little guys. They are uniquely evolved to cope with the challenging winter environment and, on average, they have a five per cent greater body mass than those found on the British mainland.

The Fulmar, or *maalie*, is our most abundant breeding species of seabird in Shetland. There is barely a ledge they have not laid claim to, from the sheerest sea cliffs to inland quarries, and roadside cuttings to ancient drystone-walled buildings. Being such a familiar species here, it is hard to imagine that the first breeding record was as recently as 1878. This was on Foula, and was the first British breeding record away from the remote Atlantic islands of St Kilda.

They are the albatross of the north. If there is a bird that inspires me to wonder what it would be like to fly, this is it. I can sit for hours, mesmerised by their mastery as they soar, spin and hang in buffeting gale-force updrafts at clifftop peaks. When conditions are right, dozens can gather in what appears to be a highly sociable activity. It is here you can fully appreciate just how impressive in the air these birds are.

Often just an arm's length away, they glide by with seemingly effortless grace. Barely a movement is made to counter gusts of wind so strong we can hardly stand up in them. It looks as if they do it for fun, and apparently, they do! Eye to eye, in these wildest moments it's easy to let yourself wonder what they are thinking or how they see us.

These gatherings usually culminate in raucous conversations, often between several birds as they settle on the clifftop. With their loud and erratic cackling, few such interactions between birds intrigue me more, but what is being said we will never know.

From land we can admire and adore their ability and beauty but, until recently, we could only imagine them in their true realm over the ocean. It was a team of researchers from the University of Aberdeen, studying Fulmars on the tiny uninhabited Orkney Island, Eynhallow, who helped us to truly appreciate and understand just how in tune they are with the ocean and its elements.

Using tiny GPS and geolocating transmitters, researchers Ewan Edwards and Paul Thompson were able to track the birds' movements from the moment they left their nests. One particular male undertook an epic North Atlantic odyssey of almost 6,300km over a period of 14 days. The distance alone is remarkable, but the route even more so: from Orkney he flew northwest to the Faroe Channel, and from there far to the southwest to the Mid Atlantic Ridge – an incredible 2,415km from Orkney.

His journey back was every bit as fascinating. Tracking landward to reach southwest Ireland, he then followed the coast northward, all the way up and across to the Western Isles and onward, eventually returning to his nest, his partner, and their egg on Eynhallow. From the data received it is fascinating to see how he knew where he was going, and when and how best to get there. Through a combination of memory, his own biological compass, and the prevailing winds and weather systems, he was concise and efficient.

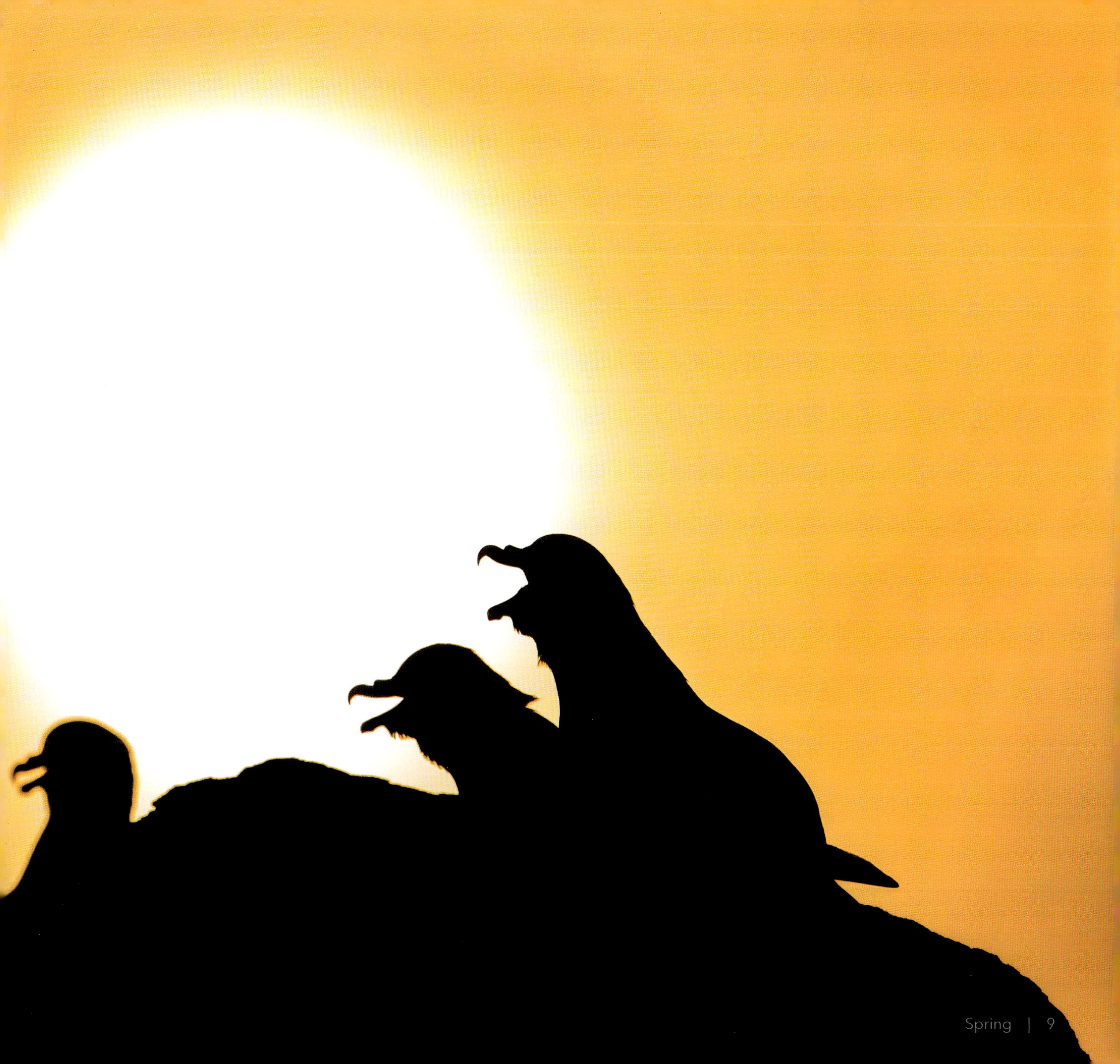

Powering through breaking waves, a mother speeds for the shore to land a small Saithe for her competitive cubs. Shetland is home to the highest density of Eurasian Otter in the British Isles and, quite probably, the world. From the renowned scientific studies carried out by Hans Kruuk almost three decades ago, through to numerous present-day production companies who come here to film them, Shetland is widely known as the best place to study Otters in the wild. Our local dialect name of *draatsi* derives from *drats* or *drittle*, which mean to move slowly or heavily, or walk in an ungainly fashion.

*"Da gale comes rivin
trow da cloods
Shestin da sea wi
michty hand,
Dies wi dir taps lekk
driven snaw
Seems desperate –
makkin fir da laand ..."*
Brakkers by John T. Hughson

The months of January and February are the windiest of the year. Gale force winds are usually expected but storm to hurricane force winds are becoming more of a feature of this time of year – 197mph being the strongest gust ever recorded. During these conditions waves of over 12m can be recorded, powered by the untamed fury of the North Atlantic Ocean. Neither words nor measurements can describe how exhilarating it is to be out in these conditions, but this picture might. It's a heady blend of exhilaration, awe and even fear that leaves no uncertainty. Never underestimate the power of the sea.

"As da days lenthen,
da cauld strengthens"

February tends to be the coldest month of the year. Being so far north it is often assumed that we have cold winters. Temperatures here however are rarely much below freezing, typically ranging between 3°C to 15°C (before wind chill) throughout the year.

Orca, or Killer Whale return to our waters relatively regularly throughout the year. Winter sightings tend to be less frequent, but can result in even more exhilarating encounters.

The spawning of frogs is a highlight in any nature calendar. Curiously though, while almost every stage of our spring exhibits a marked seasonal difference to that of elsewhere in Britain, usually being at least a fortnight behind, nobody seems to have told the frogs! Their spawning actually tends to happen at the same time as that of their counterparts elsewhere in the UK.

With neither toads nor snakes present in Shetland, the humble Common Frog is our only amphibian, though it was not originally native to the islands. Shetland's first recorded introduction took place in 1895 on my home island, Fetlar, at Brough Lodge. Further introductions took place in the 1920s in Scalloway and in Lerwick. They are now very widespread across the isles, thriving in a wide range of suitable habitats from gardens to the highest moorland.

Though the days continue to lengthen the early signs of spring are slow and subtle. For some it is the *pleepin* of Oystercatchers, or *shalders*, and the calls of Common Gulls, or *tang maas*, from the ebb, but few lift the spirits for many Shetlanders more than the sweet song of the Skylark, or *laverek*. Having wintered away in milder climates, Skylarks start to arrive back here during February.

I learned their song from my father before I even knew what one looked like, and have kept an ear to the sky for them on the first mild days of the month for as long as I can remember. Hearing that magical song while out working on the croft with my father, long before the grass had started to green, really was a talking point. It was the sign we looked forward to – *'spring wis i' da air'*.

"A laeverik high abön me - lik Palestrina sings. - As day is duly risin' - Dirs healin in his wings - Saft soonds da swill o' waater - Fur da storms at its aese" – *Joyce McDill & Freda Leask*

Confined to Northmavine, Shetland's wild and rugged northwest corner of Mainland, Purple Saxifrage is an early spring speciality and a welcome splash of colour to remind us of the botanical beauty in store during the months ahead.

As the northern hemisphere days draw out, the urge to breed grows for birds that prefer warmer winter climes, triggering a journey back to their northern breeding grounds. Along with the return of the first of our regular breeding birds, it is during this early stage of spring that we start to see the first passage migrants. The pace is invariably slow, but never mundane. The first Pied Wagtail or Woodpigeon of the year, perhaps even a Stonechat, a Mistle Thrush or a Yellowhammer – they all stir admiration for the marvel of migration.

From the boreal coniferous forests of northern Europe to a small spruce stand garden in Shetland, this Tengmalm's Owl was the first known sighting of the species in Shetland for over 120 years. Unaware of the identification or significance of their garden visitor, the hosts Jackie and Erik Moar posted a photo of their *unken peerie* owl on social media. No sooner had the picture been posted than it had been identified … and their phones started to ring …

In the modern world of social media, connectivity, and the instant sharing of imagery, discoveries like this are now intrinsically established in wildlife community culture. This was a fantastic example of how rarities can be found by anyone, at any time of the year.

Once a well-established native breeding species, the White-tailed Eagle or *erne* was one of the first birds written about in Shetland, with references to it dating back as far as 1615. Historically they were considered to be a major menace to livestock, and were relentlessly persecuted. By the 1900s Shetland's White-tailed Eagles came under yet more pressure from collectors of both specimens and eggs. The local reign of this iconic species ended in 1918 when Shetland's last surviving erne was shot in North Roe. More significantly, with that same pull of the trigger, this infamous event in our natural history also marked the extinction of White-tailed Eagle as a native British breeding species.

Thankfully, over 100 years later, changing attitudes and conservation efforts have made huge differences to some species, White-tailed Eagle amongst them. With established and successful reintroduction programmes ongoing elsewhere in the UK, and continental vagrants known to occur, sightings in the isles have increased considerably in recent years, bolstering our hopes that Shetland's former eyries may once again become occupied.

Eagles have been the subject of fact and folklore in cultures around the world for millennia. It is little wonder this should also be the case in Shetland, with the *erne* featuring in our written history for hundreds of years. In the local legend 'the eagle and the baby', a baby girl named Mary Anderson was snatched by the *erne* and carried from Norwick in Unst to an eyrie on the Blue Banks of Fetlar. It was said that the young Fetlar boy that had been lowered on ropes to rescue the baby, Robert Nicholson, married Mary many years later. As bairns, we were tantalised by this story, innocently unaware of the improbabilities of such an occurrence, or the many versions of the same story told in other cultures.

Uniquely amongst our four breeding members of the auk family, Black Guillemots, or *tysties*, are sedentary, remaining in our inshore waters year-round. Though quite a contrast to their dapper summer plumage, their frosty grey and white winter attire has its own subtle beauty. Spending much of my working life on the coast, this is a bird that I raise my binoculars for more than most, many a time to admire, but also often catching a glimpse of a splash or a ripple while watching for an Otter. Although they have a varied diet, like Otters they tend to favour bottom-feeding prey, such as Butterfish, Rockling and Scorpionfish.

A mother and her cub, silhouetted against the golden glow of sunset. Anyone who has spent a lot of time on the coast with Otters will appreciate just how special these golden-hour opportunities are.

Though familiar with our variable climate, a *moorie caavie,* or blizzard, must surely be a surprise to returning Great Skuas, or *bonxies*, having spent most of their winter at sea off the coast of northwest Africa. By April winter's grip may have eased, yet its wrath can still be felt – rarely does a spring pass without this reminder.

A few weeks behind the schedule of their breeding counterparts further south in Britain, our Puffins, or *tammie nories*, will usually start to arrive back on our cliff tops during the first week of April. Weathering the wildest storms and biggest seas, they have spent over seven months out of sight of land on the ocean. Perhaps building their confidence to return to land, they start to gather in flocks on the sea below their clifftop colonies.

As monogamous breeders, like most species of seabird they will pair for life, though they spend only the breeding season together. Once reunited on land they will rekindle pair bonds, and reclaim their summer breeding burrow.

Puffins are known to live to over 30 years of age, the oldest recorded bird being 34 years old. It's remarkable to think that from the age of five years old and then ready to breed, a bird may well spend the next 20-30 summers committed to the same partner.

Puffins have evolved to maximise the volume of prey brought back to their chick, and are able to store and carry a large number of fish in their bill, potentially dozens at a time. Inside their gape they have a series of sharp fishbone-like spines angled inwards, known as 'denticles'. This allows them to essentially skewer each fish as their bills close on them, enabling the birds to keep on grabbing more prey underwater. Like many seabirds here, sand eels were formerly very much their staple diet.

Puffins can be aged by the size, shape and pattern of their bills. Diagonal grooves running down the red portion of the bill appear with age. Usually by the time they are three years old they will show three grooves.

A fascinating discovery was made recently by ornithologist Jamie Dunning – his studies revealing that Puffins actually have glowing ultraviolet colours in their already ornate and vibrantly patterned bills. Birds are known to have far more complex retinas than humankind, and can see colours beyond those we can perceive in their plumage. It is presumed that Puffins' fluorescent beaks are most likely used as part of the breeding process and sexual selection, and may help birds to choose a prospective mate.

Steekit mist (thick fog) rolling in to cast a curtain over the Atlantic sunset.

By early spring most of the previous year's Otter families will have already separated. Cubs that have been largely dependent on their mother for the previous 10-12 months are becoming more independent, whilst their mother's instinct also starts to push them away. For these young Otters it can be a tough time. They have known nothing other than the dedication of their mother, but now face the harsh reality of the transition towards adulthood without her support.

Making things even harder, inshore fish stocks at this time are only just starting to recover from their lowest point in the year. Having known crabs as easily caught prey since around five months old, they often become something of a staple for many newly independent young Otters. Though this always looks an impressive catch, they have very low nutritional value compared to fish. In order to consume enough calories to sustain them, the young Otters must work twice as hard each day as they would catching fish.

As Shetlanders, our connection with the land and the sea runs deep. In an environment where the elements are so unreliable, the tides at least are consistent and dependable. From my early years on rock pooling adventures, going to the *craigs* to fish for *sillocks*, or heading off on a boat fishing, even as a child I learned to be in tune with the tides.

My fascination with the relationship between the tides and species became more engrained in my life as my interest in Otters grew. Though I soon learned this was not necessarily the case, I remember at one point thinking that the bigger the ebb, the better the chance of seeing Otters, and never did that prospect feel more exciting than during the spring tides at this time of year.

Otters find much of their prey at rest on the seabed, often sheltering beneath freely flowing kelp forests. With the fronds standing tall, they move with ease through them, but during low spring tides the fallen forest is as tricky for them to forage amongst as it is for us to see them in. I once had someone say to me that they were like 'little aquatic monkeys', and watching them clambering through this collapsed coastal jungle, I could see what they meant.

An old dialect name *lum* or *loomi*, is presumed to have derived from the Old Norse name lómr (meaning moaner), and gave rise to many small groups of lochans named *loomishuns* or *loomer shuns*, most of which remain favoured breeding sites to this very day.

With their evocative, mournful and eerie calls, and a synchronous, regal and elaborate dance, the Red-throated Diver, or *rain gös*, display is one of the most spectacular wildlife spectacles of the year. Side by side, and with their slender necks outstretched across the water surface, their routine begins with a haunting wail known as 'long-calling', culminating with a dramatic and beautiful synchronised dance across the water with heads bowed and wings drooped. Through folklore and place names it is clear that Red-throated Divers were as iconic to Shetlanders historically as they are today. Their distinctive flight calls as they commute back and forth from their breeding lochs to the sea were once said to foretell the weather, earning them their local name *rain gös* and forming the basis of a well-known saying:

"If da rain gös goes tae da hill,
go doo and do whit ayre doo will,

but if da rain gös goes tae da sea,
draa dee boat weel up'i da lea"

Sounds of spring. Though Shetland's breeding wader numbers are not quite what they once were, unlike those of most moor and upland habitats throughout the British Isles, our populations of the commoner species are relatively stable. Step outside into any garden away from the busy metropolises of Lerwick and Scalloway on a calm morning and you'd be surprised not to hear the beautiful bubbling song of a Curlew, or *whaap*, or the Common Snipe or *horse gok* in the distance.

Like most shorebirds of similar size, Whimbrels, or *peerie whaaps*, are strong fliers with immense stamina. Birds fitted with geo-tracking devices have been recorded making non-stop flights from their breeding grounds in Iceland to their wintering grounds in West Africa, where most of our breeding Whimbrels are also known to winter. Awareness of these epic journeys makes their return in late April all the more appreciated.

With over 90 per cent of the UK population, Shetland is the Whimbrel's British stronghold. Sadly, this is one of all too many species that, even in my brief lifespan, has declined rapidly. Throughout my childhood in the 1980s the total breeding population here was estimated to be in excess of 500 pairs, of which less than half remain.

Fetlar was the main focus of a study carried out by Murray Grant in the late 1980s, to determine effects of agricultural 'improvements' on heathland nesting habitat. My father is a relatively forward-thinking crofter and openminded to new conservation initiatives, including survey sites on our land. As a crofter-cum-naturalist this project intrigued me, particularly as it was on land I'd actually seen transformed.

We'd often meet Murray while out working, him on his Whimbrel, us on our sheep. One aspect of his work that we paid particular attention to was colour ringing. With each bird wearing a unique colour combination, he could gain a better understanding of their movements, as could we, and I remember feeling a real sense of involvement with every colour combination I reported to him. Remarkably, in 2010 one of Murray's study birds was recorded still breeding at 24 years of age – the oldest known Whimbrel in the world! But sadly, they are still declining.

"I lik ta hear da wild soonds o da nort
Whin da calloos come in near da shore,
An da tinlin-lang cry at da emmer geese gie
Whin der ready ta leave I da voar."

Da Nort by Mary Ellen Odie

Having spent the winter here in their dapper black and white plumage, Long-tailed Ducks, or *calloos*, have usually completed the pre-breeding moult into summer plumage by early May. Long-tailed Ducks have a more complex moult than any other duck, effectively changing their plumage three times in the course of the same year. It is the only living member of its genus, *Clangula*. During winter months flocks numbering into the hundreds can be seen, particularly on the stretch of water separating Unst, Yell, and Fetlar known as Bluemull Sound.

During this period of spring numbers increase as birds wintering elsewhere may also use this area as a staging post. At this time of year flocks of well over 1,000 birds can be seen which, alongside similar numbers in Orkney, represents the largest congregation of the species in Britain. By mid-month they will all have departed to their Arctic breeding grounds.

Male Wrens throughout most of their range will build as many as five or six nests within their territory. It is the female who chooses which nest and partner she will pair with. Studies have shown they usually prefer the most cryptic nests, presumably as they are the least likely to be found by predators. In Shetland where conditions are harder and densities lower, Wrens take a much more conventional approach by building only one or two nests.

A spring sunset over Da Gaada Stack, Foula. Lying 32km west of Shetland, and with an inland peak of nearly 418m, and Britain's second highest sea cliff towering 365m above sea level, the iconic outline of Foula seen on the Atlantic horizon from Mainland Shetland is as tantalising as it is dramatic. Each of Shetland's many islands has its own unique character, but Foula is on another level. Barely 13 square kilometres of landmass, dwelt upon by 30 inhabitants, Foula is a remote-island lover's dream. I am of the opinion that the phrase "awe inspiring" is overused, but it is justified in every sense to describe this island.

Though we see an interesting diversity of shorebird species here, with little in the way of estuarine habitats large congregations of them are few and far between. Occasionally, however, with certain weather conditions we can be treated to notable movements of Knot on passage. With their next stop the Arctic, migrating flocks high overhead are exciting to see. Poor visibility may even force birds to land, when flocks in the low hundreds can be seen. While not quite scenes to rival those at Snettisham in Norfolk in autumn, the colours and the spring-movement vibe can make it every bit as memorable.

Bound for the scrubby upland forest of northern Europe, but finding itself on the wrong side of the North Sea, a male Bluethroat may well be the one species that epitomises island birding in spring. May is the month during which spring passage migration is at its peak. The anticipated simple pleasures during the first half of the season are hard to beat, from the first Wheatear on an early April coastal walk to the tuneful song of a Willow Warbler in your garden. It is now that, with the appropriate weather conditions at hand, island birding can take on a more exotic hue. Though numbers and diversity of species we see are not as high as those found during autumn migration, through their song, breeding plumage, and even at times their display, spring birds whether common or rare offer a quality that autumn simply can't match.

A former British breeding species, like Bluethroat, Wryneck is a scarce spring migrant and always a highlight. A member of the woodpecker family, Wrynecks nest in holes in trees but do most of their foraging on the ground where their cryptic plumage offers them incredible camouflage.

SUMMER

With a vibrant tapestry of wildflowers, hundreds of thousands of breeding birds, and the summer sun never letting darkness fall, this is the season that captures the heart and mind like no other.

At the height of summer we see approximately 19 hours of daylight. When the sun sets we are in the land of the *simmer dim* – the twilight of a Shetland summer evening, that brief but magical period between the sun setting and rising again – when it never gets dark.

From long days spent watching the intensity of our seabird cities and the dramatic seascapes that support them, to twilight nights when the *daala mist* fills valleys and birds continue to sing, or to the gentle sparkle of an early morning dew, summer is a time that words alone cannot describe.

There has been just short of 130 species of bird recorded breeding in Shetland. Having commenced nest-building in February, the *corbie*, or Raven, is by far our earliest breeding species. As with any bird, there can be variation in timing each year, but most broods will be fledging during the second half of May.

Their dialect name is still very much in use today, but is actually of Scottish origin. Their Old Norse name, *Ramn*, a 'thieving, or dark-haired person' is no longer in use, but place names throughout the islands, such as Ramna Stacks and Ramnageo, suggest that it once was commonplace.

Renowned for their intelligence and wary nature, corbies are incredible birds to study and photograph from the secrecy of a hide in any circumstances, but particularly when they are raising chicks. Knowing the remarkable intelligence of corvids, it was intriguing to discover that the king of corvids can be tricked. With a high level of caution, planning and patience, and with someone accompanying entry and departure from the hide, even Ravens can be fooled, as they do not appear to count. As soon as the accompanying person has left, they carry on with their parenting, unaware of their hidden observer.

*"Niver cast a kloot, till
da mont o May is oot"*

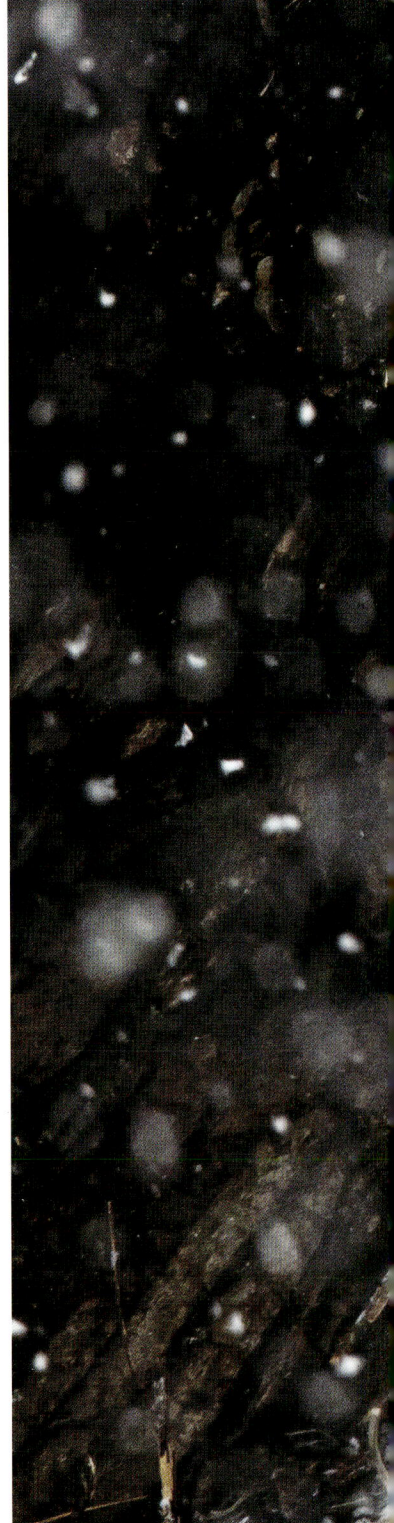

May scarcely passes without one last reminder of winter. Usually it will be little more than a hail or sleet shower, but as a well-known Shetland version of the Scottish saying explicitly warns, be wary of shedding layers until after May!

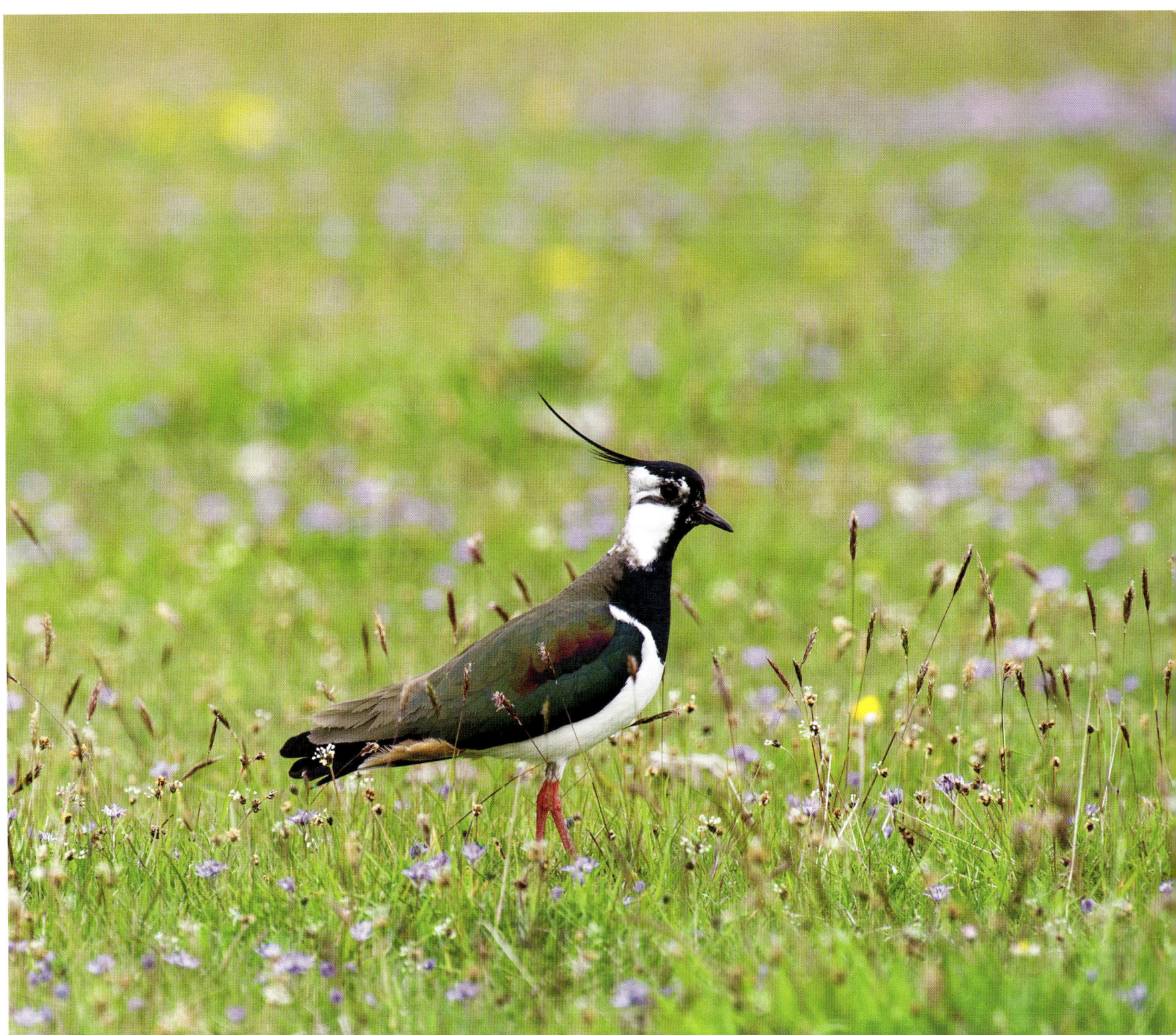

Tieve's nacket, or Lapwing, on herb-rich serpentine heath, with flowering Spring Squill, a flower that characterises this and many coastal habitats during this stage of spring.

With partially webbed feet and an elegant build, the Red-necked Phalarope is a well-adapted surface swimmer and they spend the majority of their time on the water. It is thanks to this that they are known on Fetlar as the *peerie deuck*, a name also given to Teal elsewhere in Shetland, meaning 'small duck'. In addition to their charisma, attractive plumage and fascinating behaviour, they are also marvellously confiding.

Formerly, they were very much regarded as a Fetlar speciality, and so they were a much-loved bird on the island. Their return in May was as much a talking point in the community as the first lark to sing or new-born lamb. It is a species that lies in the very roots of my love of nature.

The Red-necked Phalarope is an abundant breeding species across its range in the Arctic regions of Europe, Asia and North America. Here in Britain, however, it is a very rare breeder on the very southern fringe of its breeding range.

Following a decline in the population during the late 1990s and early 2000s, extensive habitat management, along with the co-operation of local landowners and the dedication of former Royal Society for the Protection of Birds (RSPB) wardens such as Malcie Smith and Dave Suddaby, saw the population begin to increase, a trend which continues today through site manager Kevin Kelly and many others.

Recent years have seen an exciting rise in numbers, with new sites discovered elsewhere in the isles. However, Fetlar, which used to account for over 95 per cent of the entire British breeding population, is still very much their UK stronghold.

Not much larger than a bumblebee, the chicks hatch after approximately 17-20 days incubation. Like most wader chicks they are precocial, meaning they can feed themselves, and they leave the nest soon after hatching. They will be guarded by the male and fully fledged less than two weeks after they hatched.

Of all the fascinating information to arise from the work done with Fetlar's phalaropes, finding where our birds spend the winter was the most remarkable discovery of all. In 2012, the former RSPB Scotland warden Malcie Smith, who spent two decades working on the species, led a pioneering project in association with the Swiss Ornithological Institute and the Shetland Ringing Group in which they fitted geolocators to several 'phals' on Fetlar's breeding marshes.

The following summer, data was recovered from a returned male bird revealing that he had spent the winter in the warm tropical waters between the Galapagos Islands, mainland Ecuador, and Peru – meaning he had undergone a staggering 25,750km journey to the Pacific Ocean and back again! This was the first time a journey to South America had been recorded for a European breeding bird. Geolocators from a further two males, showing very similar routes, were recovered in 2017.

It had long been known through sightings and recoveries of ringed birds that Red-necked Phalaropes breeding in the North American Arctic wintered off western South America, and that Scandinavian Arctic breeding birds wintered in the Arabian Sea. However, the wintering location of birds from Greenland, Iceland and Shetland was unknown.

The revelation of the wintering quarters of Shetland's phalaropes prompted similar studies to be undertaken on phalaropes breeding in Greenland, Iceland, Norway, Sweden, Finland and Russia. This work confirmed that the wider Atlantic breeding population was divided into two migratory populations, and showed that birds breeding in Shetland, Iceland and Greenland wintered in the Pacific, while the more eastern populations wintered in the Arabian Sea.

Sunrise and the delicate sparkles of early morning dew.

In June 2018, when this magnificent sea mammal was discovered in Skerries, it was huge news. This young male had first appeared in Orkney in March, having presumably travelled approximately 3,200km from the nearest colonies in Svalbard, and put in several appearances along the west coast of Scotland. As the first Walrus to be recorded in Shetland in several decades, it was a chance not to be missed.

Annual UK sightings in subsequent years have afforded nature lovers incredible opportunities to see this Arctic icon. While immature Walruses have a history of wandering, there may be a darker side to recent records. Rising sea temperature generated by global warming is reducing the Arctic ice edge upon which the species depends. Some scientists have speculated that this reduction in suitable habitat may be causing some animals to wander more widely.

Formerly a great rarity in Britain, White-billed Diver was once regarded as a Shetland winter speciality. Spring is now peak time for the chance to find this enigmatic High Arctic breeding species and, in their summer splendour, there are few finer looking birds.

To think that this delicate little flower grows nowhere else in the world other than the serpentine debris of Unst really is pretty amazing. That it was discovered in 1837 by 12-year-old Thomas Edmondston is truly extraordinary. In that same year, this remarkable young naturalist compiled the first ever known list of Shetland's plants, followed in 1845 by the publication of the *Flora of Shetland*. As an eminent family of their time, the Edmondstons' work and achievements give an invaluable insight into Shetland and its natural history.

Thomas went on to be appointed Professor of Botany at Anderson University in Glasgow and was a regular correspondent of Charles Darwin. Tragically though, just a few months later, his short life and blossoming career ended in tragedy when he was fatally wounded disembarking the HMS *Herald* off the coast of South America.

Recorded at only three sites in the British Isles, the 7-11mm long Leaf Beetle (*Chrysolina intermedia*), also known as Plantain Leaf Beetle, is rare. In Shetland it has only been recorded on the Keen of Hamar, where even there it is restricted to just a few small areas of serpentine debris. Surprisingly little is known about it, making it as intriguing as it is arresting. Curiously, DNA research carried out in Shetland, Orkney and Argyll revealed that although their habitat choices were completely different at each location, they were all found to be of the same species.

A brood of newly-hatched Skylark chicks. Many species of passerines have patterned tongues and brightly coloured gapes to help parents target their hungry mouths when feeding in shadowed, partially-hidden nests.

With wings outstretched, and in full voice, the iconic display of the mighty Great Skua, or *bonxie,* characterised summer on the hills to me as a child more than any other. There were plenty of prettier birds to look at and to listen to, but the bonxie was big, powerful and renowned for its fearless nature. Our dialect name is thought to have derived from the Norse word *bunksi*, a word used to describe a 'stout ill-tempered man'.

Bonxies were first officially recorded breeding here in 1774. A charismatic species, their history is as turbulent as it is fascinating, encompassing the pioneering conservation efforts of Laurence Edmondston in the 1830s to protect them from 'collectors' on Hermaness, through to their subsequent remarkable population expansion.

Prior to 2021, the entire world population (confined to the northeast Atlantic) was estimated to be upwards of 16,000 breeding pairs – a remarkable 60 per cent of which was found in Scotland – with Shetland alone accounting for almost 40 per cent of the global population.

During breeding seasons of 2021 and 2022 an unimaginable tragedy swept through Scotland's breeding population as a highly pathogenic avian influenza (HPAI), also known as bird flu, swept through the colonies. During these two breeding seasons alone, a catastrophic 80-85 per cent has been lost to this horrendous virus.

With such a devastating loss in such a short time, it is not yet clear what the future holds for this powerful and resilient species, though at least in the 2023 breeding season there appeared to be no evidence of the virus amongst them.

Bonxies famously gather in large numbers to bathe in lochs close to large colonies. These congregations tend to consist of off-duty breeding birds whilst 'club sites' are gatherings of non-breeding immature birds.

"O simmer dim, O simmer dim!
I canna sleep avaa.
Du sheens in trow my window bright
An pits da sleep awaa ..."

Simmer Dim by R.W. Isbister

In Shetland the largest colonies are found at Hermaness, Saxa Vord and Foula, which as recently as the turn of the 21st century was the largest colony of their kind in the world. Old accounts from visitors to the island noted that not only was there a trade in bonxie specimens and eggs, but they were also used as a food source by the islanders. A chick ringed here on 15th July 1979 was found dead 38 years later, also on 15th July, in the Netherlands, which is thought to be the longest-lived bonxie in the world. An even more interesting discovery was a Shetland-raised bonxie found breeding in northern Russia.

From a young age I witnessed on our croft what might be described as their more brutal side, particularly during lambing. Even then I saw beyond the damage they could inflict and admired them. Over time I learned just how adaptable a species they are, and just how varied their dietary, foraging and hunting strategies are. Currently, the majority of bonxies feed on discards from the fishing industry, catching sand eels (when available) and, especially, by robbing Gannets of their catch – a behaviour known as kleptoparasitism, which means that they rob what other species have caught for themselves. Then, there is the small percentage of bonxies that specialise in living by catching other seabirds.

These predators have had detrimental effects on many colonies and often specialise on one particular species – Puffin being this particular pair's food of choice. Watching from a favoured grassy knoll over the cliffs below, pairs like these lay claim to specific hunting ranges. The sight of flocks of terrified Puffins scattering off the slopes is a familiar occurrence when they launch an attack.

However unfair or brutal these hunting strategies may appear to some, this is the harsh reality between predator and prey – they are simply striving to provide for their own.

Markedly smaller, more streamlined, eye-catching and agile, many might argue Arctic Skua, or *skootie alan*, is a more attractive bird than Great Skua. Like Pomarine and Long-tailed Skua, Arctic has pale and light morph plumages. In North American English these three smaller skuas are known as jaegers, which derives from the German word *jäger*, meaning 'hunter'. The scientific name for all seven species of skuas is *Stercorarious* and means 'of dung'. This curiously stems from the old belief that the food disgorged by birds they chased was excrement, not regurgitated or dropped food!

This is put fantastically in context by a minister, John Brand, who visited Shetland in 1700 and who was clearly quite taken by the *skootie alan:*

> There is a fowl called the *scutiallan*, of a black colour and as big as a wild duck, which doth live upon the vomit and excrement of other fowls whom they pursue and having apprehended them, they cause them to vomit up what they have taken and not yet digested: The Lord's Work both of Nature and Grace are wonderful, all speaking forth his glorious Goodness, Wisdom and Power.

Arctic Skuas are masters of kleptoparasitism, depending hugely on the feeding success of other seabirds. For millennia they have depended upon the fortunes of thousands of terns, Puffins and Kittiwakes, without which they cannot provide enough food to raise their own chicks. Since the crash of the sand eel populations there have been several decades of decline but, at last, over the past couple of years we are starting to see chicks fledging successfully again.

The aerial assault on Arctic Terns from these charismatic skuas is a remarkable sight. Terns returning from foraging trips with sand eels are singled out, attacked and eventually robbed in the most spectacular show of aerial agility. The fast pace and manoeuvrability of both species is perfectly matched – however the persistent harassment by the skua usually sees them victorious.

With barely a chick raised for decades, to see breeding success slowly returning for Arctic Skuas has been one of the greatest joys of recent years. With the population plummeting from over 1,000 pairs in the early 1990s to a low point of barely 200 pairs, their recent success restores hope for our superlative *skootie alans*.

Known locally as the *tirrik*, the Arctic Tern is a special bird to Shetlanders. Although they do not return until May, it is seen by many as the true herald of the islands' summer. Their arrival date each year shows remarkable consistency, almost to the day, as they start to arrive between the 5th and 7th of May.

Their return is all the more appreciated when we think of the journey they have undertaken. Spending their summer in high latitudes and their winter way down in the southern hemisphere, *tirriks* see more summer sun and undertake a longer migration than any other bird in the world.

While their amazing annual 'pole to pole' migration has long been known, recent studies revealed that their epic journey is even more remarkable than we suspected. A ground-breaking study led by Newcastle University, in collaboration with *BBC Springwatch* and the National Trust, involved birds breeding on the Farne Islands off the Northumbrian coast. Geolocators fitted during the breeding season revealed that some of these birds, weighing just over 100g, had flown a distance of up to 90,100km by the time they had returned.

It wasn't only the epic distances recorded that were so impressive, but also the information obtained about their route and behaviour during the journey. The geolocators showed that, before beginning the journey to Antarctica, some of these birds took an overland detour across Ireland and then out into the Atlantic. They were recorded to fly for as many as 24 days nonstop, feeding on the wing as they went.

Although such a study has not been undertaken in Shetland, it is quite likely that our birds will travel the same distances and take a similar route. What is most staggering of all is to think that, as Arctic Terns have been known to live as long as 32 years, in the course of their lifetime they could potentially fly the equivalent distance to the moon and back nearly four times!

In the early 1980s it was estimated that there were over 30,000 breeding pairs. Swarming, noisy and often angry skies, if near a breeding colony, were once a spectacle that characterised the summer to many a Shetlander.

It is sobering to think that the total Shetland population now amounts to little more than the biggest colonies back in my childhood days of 4,000 pairs. It was a crash in sand eel population that triggered a dramatic decline, which initially was blamed solely on overfishing. It eventually became clear that although this was a contributing factor, the problem was much more serious. Rising sea temperature from global warming was having a much greater impact, weakening the vital links in the overall marine ecosystem food chain and effecting sand eel population and distribution.

It is encouraging to see efforts still being made to protect the vital sand eel populations through government-enforced fishing bans in the UK, and what would be even more encouraging is for the same positive action to be taken by all European countries.

By targeting different prey, such as juvenile Saithe, Arctic Terns have been trying to adapt over recent years and have at last been enjoying some breeding success.

Spending their summer in high latitudes and their winter way down in the southern hemisphere, *tirriks* see more summer sun and undertake a longer migration than any other bird.

"Whaar idder flooers wid pine an dowe,
An very little else could growe,
Du wadders wind an brakkin sea,
An lifts dy head triumphantly,
Spreads beauty oot alang da aidge,
O da grey an barren rocky laidge."

Sea Pinks by Rhoda Bulter

One of our nicest sounding dialect names is *sandiloo* , the name for Ringed Plover. We are fortunate here to have a fairly healthy breeding population. They are widespread across a variety of habitats from the shingle beaches of our coastal edges up to the stony debris of the highest hills.

Many species of wading birds have special adaptations to help them find and catch their food, such as extra nerves in the tips of their bills, or an ability to open long beaks while probed into mud, but the *sandiloo* hunts by sight.

From the coast to the clifftops, the Sea Pink, or *banksflooer*, is the flower that characterises midsummer on the shores of Shetland. As Otters spend most of their active hours on the seaweed-carpeted shore, or foraging beyond it, it is not always easy to capture seasonal context in photographs. With patience, learning their routines, and especially how and when they use every nook and cranny of their territory, you can build a better picture of their fascinating lives, such as this male leaving his 'lay-up'.

Many lay-ups used by Otters are on small, sometimes inaccessible islets and vegetated outcrops and stacks. These are areas upon which, during long summer days and particularly at high tide, Otters will groom and rest, often sleeping for several hours.

One of just five species of butterfly regularly recorded here, Painted Lady is one of the world's most common and widely distributed species. In Britain they are an irruptive migrant, arriving from Africa via Europe each summer in varying numbers. Whether they returned to Africa was a matter of conjecture, until an astonishing recent discovery was made.

Rader technology revealed that those Painted Ladies that emerge in northern Europe in late summer migrate, at an average height of over 500m, well out of sight of us or potential predators, all the way back to the regions of tropical Africa that their grandparents (or great-grandparents) originated from earlier in the year.

Known in Shetland as *alamootie*, the European Storm-petrel is the smallest seabird in the Atlantic. Weighing just 25g, little bigger than a sparrow, it is hard to comprehend just how extreme a life this bird lives. For all they appear fragile, they endure atrocious and even violent conditions out on the ocean realm far from the sight of land.

To see these enigmatic birds takes effort. On land, you must adjust to their nocturnal activities. At sea you need to go where they go. Out in their ocean realm, in contrast to the haste they need over land at night, they appear graceful and elegant, flitting over the water as if tiptoeing as they glean food from just beneath the surface. Out there, in their element, you appreciate all the more how special these birds are. We can only be there by engine and radar, and only comfortably in the calmest of conditions, whilst they wander these waves in even the most challenging weather.

As is the case with all seabirds, 'stormies' return to land only to breed. Nesting in crevices, cracks and holes in remote coastal colonies, they must leave and return from offshore feeding grounds under cover of darkness. Their small and dainty size make them particularly vulnerable to predators on land, including gulls and skuas.

Along with shearwaters and albatross, petrels belong to the order of birds known as *Procellariiformes*. The family group is also referred to as tubenoses: they all have remarkably well-adapted nostrils which help them locate food over vast distances by sense of smell alone.

Spending their summers here, they migrate south to winter in the South Atlantic, mainly off South Africa and Namibia. They have a pelagic lifestyle, spending most of their time flitting over the waves, dancing over the surface with a pitter-patter motion as they peck for planktonic foods, scraps of ocean life so small we can barely see them. When foraging during the breeding season they may be at sea for as many as four days, and they are able to convert their microscopic catch into a rich, oily, and highly calorific stomach liquid.

On dry land there is one particularly special place to experience stormies – the small uninhabited island of Mousa, estimated to be home to over 11,000 breeding pairs. Late-night summer excursions to the island and its remarkable Iron Age broch, standing over 12m high, are not to be missed. This is one of the most studied Storm-petrel colonies in Europe. Three decades of research carried out by Mark Bolton (RSPB Principal Conservation Scientist) has revealed some fascinating discoveries about their breeding ecology.

Fitting tiny GPS tracking devices, Mark Bolton discovered that breeding adults from the colony were regularly recorded travelling 200-300km in search of food. One particular bird however, presumably swept by strong westerly winds recorded at the time, travelled 400km east to the coast of Norway. For just a few hours overnight it lingered in a fjord just north of Stavanger, apparently avoiding the weather, but it was back with its chick 24 hours later.

As a child, being told of this mysterious, tiny, sparrow-sized seabird that flew at night like a bat, walked on water at sea, and nested in the wildest cliffs of your home island meant I just had to see it. Thanks to the kindness of RSPB wardens Nick Dymond and the late Mike Peacock, I had enjoyed late-night expeditions to colonies on some of Fetlar's most dramatic cliffs before I was even 10 years old.

Gazing skyward into the twilight from the gentle slopes of boulder-scree cliffs we'd catch glimpses of their bat-like form whizzing past in a blur, whilst hearing their captivating churring calls (which Bobby Tulloch had humorously described as "the sound of fairies being sick") from amongst the rocks around us was mysterious and magical. Up close and personal, when in the hand they are even more compelling – their strangely sweet, musky smell combined with such delicate and dainty proportions.

The Shetland Bird Club emblem. The *tystie*, or Black Guillemot, is unique amongst its local breeding auk relatives in laying not one, but two eggs. They have a preference to nest in loose colonies, usually consisting of little more than a dozen or so pairs tucked amongst boulder screes, crevices or burrows along lower-lying coastlines. Their colonies may lack the drama of the breathtaking cliffs favoured by their cousins but, with regular displays and disputes, their social lives can be every bit as entertaining.

Instead of seeking shoaling fish in high volume they prefer to forage for inshore bottom-feeding species such as Butterfish, Eelpout, Rockling and flatfish – all very similar prey preference to Otters here. Young Saithe, better known here as *sillocks*, are also a favourite prey for them.

The *rippik maa,* or Kittiwake, is one of the most successful and widespread gulls in the northern hemisphere. Though elegant in appearance they are notoriously feisty and competitive, arguing over the best nest sites on precarious cliff ledges. Nests are generally much closer together than those of ground-nesting gulls. The few suitable ledges found on the sheer cliff faces of their colonies are in high demand and aggressively defended.

As has been the case for other sand eel dependent seabirds, the Kittiwake population has plummeted over recent decades, but there are new signs of hope for the rippik maa. This tenacious little gull has recently enjoyed its most successful breeding seasons in well over a decade. Though it is too soon to know, the success shown amongst this and several other species of seabird in recent years does suggest things are slowly improving, and new generations may hopefully enjoy more prosperous times.

Known in Shetland as *lungvie,* the Common Guillemot may not be as glamorous in appearance as a *tammie norie*, but they are every bit as impressive in terms of performance. Capable of diving to depths of 180m beneath the surface of the ocean in search of prey, submerged for up to four and a half minutes, they are supreme underwater predators.

This is a long-lived seabird, many living well into their thirties. The oldest known was a remarkable 43 years old. Like most other seabirds they don't breed until they are five years old. Once they become an established parent, they will return to the same tiny space on a crammed nesting sea-cliff ledge year after year. So tightly positioned are they that, in the busiest colonies, there can be as many as 20 pairs in just one square metre.

As monogamous breeders, pairs will have a wonderfully committed and attentive bond. Unlike many seabirds, they not only have a mutual tolerance to one another – literally rubbing shoulders with their neighbours summer after summer – but their caring nature also extends to those 'next door' in the colony, and so mutual preening occurs regularly.

A fascinating recent study revealed that the Guillemot's conical egg shape was not actually about safety, but more likely, hygiene. Contrary to the belief that the pear-like shape was to reduce the chances of the egg rolling off the ledge, research by Tim Birkhead suggests it is about the egg, and developing chick inside being able to breath. The pyramidal shape means that the tapering, longer cone end of the egg remains flat on the ledge but, the rounded broadest end is not in contact with the guano layered ledges and remains relatively clean, so allowing the egg to breathe.

Before they have even fledged, the chicks leave their ledges with a dramatic and quite astonishing leap to the sea below, which has led to them being nicknamed 'jumplings'. Encouraged by the eerie cries of their father waiting for them on the sea, and driven by an undeniable instinct, the chicks jump from the safety of their nest ledge. Descending in freefall to the sea below, some even bounce off the rocks of the cliff face as they tumble down. Remarkably, they are rarely known to injure themselves.

It's hard to imagine this compelling instinct – they must leave the only thing they have ever known, their life on the ledge, and learn that the sea is now their safe haven. By this stage the father has been left with the sole parental responsibility, mum having already left the colony for the open ocean. Once on the water, the father hurriedly reunites with his tiny chick and wastes no time in shepherding his charge to the relative safety of the open ocean.

Unlike Guillemots and Razorbills, when the time comes for the Puffin chick to fledge, it must do so alone. When the parents feel the chick is ready, they simply stop returning to the burrow and their parental work ends. After a day or so of no feeding visits, the 'puffling' is drawn out by instinct (and presumably hunger). It leaves the safety of the burrow and it throws itself seaward. Once on the water, driven by that same incredible instinct, its little legs paddle it seaward until out on the ocean where it will remain until the following summer. As if this is not mind-blowing enough, without being shown what to do by a parent, it instinctively knows to dive for prey.

By late July in Shetland breeding *tammie nories* are at their busiest. Their single chick will fledge after about 40 days. On average they will be fed about half a dozen times per day, however, feeds usually double in frequency during their fourth week with parents having been known to make as many as 26 visits in a day. Some studies have estimated that during the six-week chick-rearing term the young could consume over 2,000 fish!

In 2017 'Project Puffin', an extensive survey carried out by the RSPB, found that populations had declined by at least 42 per cent, perhaps even as much as 60 per cent in some colonies. To census the population the RSPB used the same methodology at the same sites as had been undertaken in the last study, 15 years before, to help gain a consistent estimate.

The team also carried out some fascinating studies by fitting GPS tracking devices to adult chick-rearing Puffins. This pioneering aspect of the project revealed where the birds from a Hermaness colony in Unst foraged when they left their burrows. One headed out into the North Atlantic, another appeared to specialise inshore and circumnavigated the island, whilst another ranged east almost halfway to Norway. The most remarkable, however, was the individual which travelled over 400km to feed. These erratic geographic patterns, along with the lengthy time they were away at sea and the small catches of poorer-quality fish, differed significantly to a similar study carried out on the Shiant Isles, off the west coast of Scotland, where birds were making far shorter foraging trips.

Similar tracking studies on the island of Skomer recently revealed that Puffins set out on individually unique journeys for the winter. What was really fascinating was that although there were many different wintering strategies, each individual more or less followed the same pattern each year before returning to breed.

The most successful and busy colonies are those where the Puffins are travelling shorter distances to find food. Photographs of Puffins carrying food which have been sent by citizen scientists to the RSPB's 'puffarazzi' project suggest they might also be catching more varied, and larger prey.

From the Storm Petrel colonies of Mousa broch, to the penguin rookeries of Antarctica, to albatross encounters off New Zealand, I am lucky to have enjoyed seabirds in some truly epic environments, but few can match the atmosphere of a Hermaness gannetry at the height of the *simmer dim*.

The Northern Gannet, known in Shetland as the *solan gös*, is one of the most successful and prolific seabirds in the northern hemisphere. In uplifting contrast to the decline witnessed in so many seabird species, Gannets buck the trend. So successful are they across the North Atlantic that they show a consistent population increase of around two per cent per year.

With such success and abundance here, it is hard to imagine that they have only been breeding here since 1914 when a single pair nested on the cliffs of Noss, followed by a few pairs establishing themselves on Hermaness in 1917. These two sites remain the islands' strongholds, with only two other colonies establishing since, on the outer islands of Foula and Fair Isle.

With at least two nests per square metre, and breeding pairs potentially numbering into the tens of thousands, it is little wonder that the expression 'seabird city' is so widely known today. Gannets have a preference to nest in the most remote, awe-inspiring and, to us, inhospitable environments. Few colonies exemplify these qualities better than the cliffs and sea stacks of Hermaness.

Gannets do not start to breed until they are five years old and are generally considered monogamous breeders. They have been known to live up to 37 years old and so, in theory, could potentially form relationships lasting two, even three decades. Courtship is a key factor to maintaining such a pair bond, and it continues throughout the season, as does the gifting of material to line the nest.

Immature birds generally don't spend much time in colonies during their first couple of years. Satellite tracking research carried out by Professor Steve Votier and his team, however, logged one particular individual visiting ten different colonies in the northeast Atlantic in just one week.

To us, that turn of phrase puts the hustle and bustle of these high-density populations into a context we understand, and yet it is telling how out of place we still feel in their proximity.

Prior to the tragic losses suffered during the 2022 avian influenza pandemic (otherwise known as bird flu) they had an estimated UK breeding population of around 300,000 breeding pairs, over 40,000 of which breed on Shetland.

Although some colonies lost as much as 40 per cent of breeding birds during that season, by 2023 there was already very positive signs of recovery, some suggestions that the species appeared to be building an immunity to the virus.

In gale-force updrafts, Gannets' mastery of the air becomes all the more astonishing. Soaring over their colonies, they often strike some interesting synchronization, as if in planned flight formation.

Perhaps one of the most familiar and impressive of foraging techniques of any bird, diving Gannets may reach speeds up to 50mph before they enter the water. At these speeds, from as high as 50m above the water's surface, they can penetrate as deep as 15m beneath the surface to reach prey and, with underwater wing beats to maintain their momentum, have been known to reach depths of 30m.

To achieve this, Gannets are highly adapted. Firstly, and before they dive, they must locate their prey by sight. They have intensely clear and pale irises with minute pupils. Their eyes are able to switch from aerial to underwater vision, and they also have a flexible sclera which allows for changes in pressure during diving.

They do not have nostrils in the conventional sense, but breathe through thin slits where the upper mandible meets the skull, which are covered by a flap of hard tissue that closes when the bird strikes the water. To cope with the impact as their 3kg body hits the water at 25m per second, their sturdily reinforced skull is cushioned with pockets of air which are inflated to act as shock absorbers.

There are few better ways to appreciate these adaptations and the extraordinary spectacle than out on the sea, amidst a feeding frenzy off the island of Noss. Richard Shucksmith's underwater imagery from this location over a decade ago offered a fascinating insight into their underwater world, now a highly sought after photographic assignment.

It's a sobering reality that more Gannet nests now contain marine plastic debris than those that don't. Fisheries-related waste, with off-cuts of ropes and netting being preferred by nesting Gannets, result in entanglement and significant mortality rates every summer. Building on the same nest each year, some nests may be up to a metre tall. In one particular colony, a study by Steve Votier and a team from the University of Plymouth found the average nest contained 469.91g of plastic, equating to a staggering estimated colony total of 18.46 tonnes.

An even greater threat to seabirds and marine mammals is the ingestion of microplastics. Through the entire marine ecosystem, from the smallest fish to the largest cetacean, plastic particles are being inadvertently consumed, whilst some species, such as the tubenoses (albatross, shearwaters, Fulmars and petrels) forage primarily by smell and mistake some plastics for food due to their odour being similar to that emitted by their natural foods.

More Orca sightings are recorded in Shetland each year than from any other location in the British Isles. Though they are not considered resident they can be seen in any month of the year, with recognised peaks for occurrence. Several pods have been identified here, however most sightings relate to the same regular pods – the 65s, 64s, and the 27s, the latter being most regularly seen in recent years.

From the absence of historic references, dialect names, or written accounts, it is clear this has not long been the case. As a child we never really heard of 'Killer Whales'. It wasn't until my mid-teens that I first saw them. I will never forget that moment – the bull's dorsal fin cutting up out of the calm sea, as the pod surfaced just metres from the rock armour of the Fetlar ferry terminal, the moment was so exhilarating and exotic, it barely felt real.

Orca are found throughout all the world's oceans and are generally considered a single species (*Orcinus orca*) which in some regions are divided into ecotypes – these are ecologically and genetically distinct populations. Their behaviour and movements are essentially defined by diet and generally divided into two groups – 'transient' or 'resident', each with their own distinctive hunting strategies. The former are supreme predators, usually migratory, that primarily hunt marine mammals; whilst the latter, as their name suggests, tend to stay in one area and feed on fish.

In contrast, the pods which visit Shetland to hunt seals each summer are known to spend much of the winter feeding on Herring off Iceland. Much is still to be learned of these magnificent sea mammals but understanding is increasing through photo identification. Well over 1,000 individuals have now been identified and catalogued by research teams in Iceland, Norway and Scotland. As many as half a dozen pods, comprising as many as 40 identifiable individuals, have been recorded inshore here in Shetland in work initiated by research biologist Dr Andy Foote. Andy and his colleagues were able to confirm that the same individuals were returning to Shetland year after year, and to chart their movements throughout the rest of the year. Thankfully this work continues today, expanded upon by a growing citizen science network, in Shetland and beyond.

Killer Whales are also seasonally observed feeding upon mackerel around Shetland, with a distinct population thought to feed predominantly on this prolific food source. This population has learned to utilise the industrial fishing industry, as some Herring feeders also have. Remarkably, the animals appear to have learned to respond to the changing acoustic signal of engines made by the ships as they begin to haul their nets and, like we would respond to a dinner bell, they use this as a cue to approach and investigate the fishing boats for easy pickings that overspill the tightening nets.

There has also been some fascinating work done on Orca acoustics here, carried out by Dr Volker Deeke, who joined the team in 2009 to research vocal behaviour of these whales and how it related to diet and different groups. I was very fortunate to be invited out to join them on the boat, some three-four nautical miles west of Muckle Flugga.

Remarkably, by using a hydrophone to listen for their vocalisations underwater, we were able to locate the Orca by picking up their calls. Donning the headphones, listening to Orca we couldn't even see was totally surreal. Eventually, once their direction was established, it was the tell-tale sign of a feeding frenzy of Gannets that allowed us to home in on their precise location.

Their hunting strategy was incredible to watch, particularly when associated with several hundred Gannets. Herring like to remain deep in the water during the day. To reach them the Orca must dive to herd and force them back to the surface, a strategy known as carousel feeding. When doing so everything went quiet, even the Gannets stopped diving but continued to circle patiently overhead, presumably able to see what was unfolding below them.

In contrast to the silence and stealth of seal hunting, when herding the Herring the Orca use specific low frequency 'moan-like' vocalisations which are thought to vibrate the Herrings' swim bladders, causing them to shoal together and move towards the surface. To listen to this taking place in the depths below was incredible, whilst everything around us at the surface was quiet.

Then, eventually, streams of bubbles and ghostly shapes appeared as the gathered bait ball of Herring appeared from the depths. Suddenly, chaos! The frenzy peaked as the Herring reached the surface, the two marine predators cashing in on the bounty – Orca from below, and Gannets from above.

Often measuring over 1.5m tall, the dorsal fin of a bull Orca is surely the most recognisable fin in the ocean. Fully grown, bulls in our 'North Atlantic community' can measure nearly seven metres in length and weigh well over five tonnes, and on average are expected to live around 50-60 years. At top speed they can reach around 56km per hour and they may travel well over 80km in the course of a day. Mothers, or cows, will usually only calve once every five years, and sub-adult females within the close-knit group are known to share the childcare roles during the first few years.

What's in a name – Orca or Killer Whale? There are some who hold the view that 'Killer Whale' gives the species an unfair or misleading reputation, as there is a negative connotation associated with the word 'killer'. The irony of this is that the scientific name *Orcinus orca*, promoted by some as a less judgemental name, comes from the mythical Roman god of death, Orcus.

They are highly intelligent marine predators which display many sophisticated hunting strategies, from tipping seals off Antarctic ice floes, snatching Sea Lions off Argentinian beaches, hunting Grey Whales off California, even taking on the formidable Great White Shark off South Africa. Whatever their prey, it should neither make them more nor less appealing to us. Their adaptable, varied predatory lifestyles do not make them any less beautiful or intelligent – they simply make them more fascinating and intriguing.

Dunter (Common Eider) mums are well known for their sociable parenting. The crèches they form with their broods of ducklings in sheltered bays in summer are a real delight. Generally, they nest inland and are semi-colonial breeders, tending to nest at the same site year after year. During incubation the mother will not feed, and will only leave her clutch every two or three days to drink. Females within these communities form close-knit social structures and are known to share the responsibilities of caring for their broods.

Shetland is home to more than half the UK's entire breeding population of Red-throated Diver. As shy birds the plethora of lochs and small lochans across our remote and undisturbed upland habitats are ideal breeding sites, whilst the inshore waters in which they feed are an easy commute.

Divers, or loons as they are also known, are supremely adapted for underwater foraging and long-distance flights. They are large birds but have a comparatively small wingspan. Like shags, cormorants and grebes, they are specialist foot-propelled swimmers that can make fast and sharp manoeuvres to catch prey. When foraging, Red-throats can dive for one and a half minutes or more, their dense bones enabling longer dives, but this weight comes at an energetic cost while airborne, meaning they must beat their wings constantly while in flight.

Like many seabirds, sand eels are the *rain gös's* favourite prey, although *sillocks* (juvenile Saithe) do make up a large percentage of their diet these days. In a single day, parents can make as many as 15 or more foraging trips in search of food for their chicks. Incubation takes up to 26 days but from hatching the chick will take up to 43 days to fledge. Adults will stay with them for the first few weeks on the sea where, at first, they continue to provision them with prey while they learn to forage for themselves.

Red-throated Divers are unique amongst our dive-feeding seabirds in their upland breeding habits, yet they feed exclusively at sea – only exceptionally will they forage on larger freshwater lochs.

Weighing up to 2kg and capable of reaching top flight speed of up to 48mph, their return flight is spectacular. With outstretched wings, their massive feet trailing like the landing gear on a seaplane, they hit the water with a dramatic explosion of water droplets on impact.

So well adapted are they for their aerial and underwater environment, they are barely able to walk or even stand upright on land. Due to this, they must nest right on the water's edge, which can leave them vulnerable to their nest flooding in the event of rising water levels. Conversely, in the drier summers, if water levels fall too low they may not have the depth to dive to avoid predators, or have sufficient distance of water surface to land and take off.

Interestingly, there are occasions when adults will lead their chicks short distances overland from their small breeding lochans to larger bodies of water. Using their powerful legs to push them, they manage to shove and slide themselves over the moorland.

Unlike other species of diver that nest on large lakes, Red-throats prefer (and are more successful) on smaller lochans and pools. They are ready to breed at five years old and generally pair for life. Once they have established a suitable breeding loch they are fiercely territorial. During late summer especially, tensions can run high as young and newly-formed prospecting pairs often compete to overthrow residents. Launching torpedo-style assaults on the assailants under the water, the defending birds' defence can be super-charged, aggressive and spectacular.

But the interlopers can be equally as ferocious. I've watched unguarded chicks so relentlessly pursued by the drowning attempts launched by their attackers that they've actually had to clamber out of the water and onto the bank to hide on the moor, only returning when the coast was clear.

True to form for all seabirds, they are long-lived birds. A long-running ringing study in Shetland has revealed that they may live for over three decades, with the oldest known to be 32 years of age. Among many other findings, this same study has also shown that males usually return to breed to the same areas that they were hatched, although females may wander more to find a breeding lochan.

*"You see da luckaminnie's oo
In hentins spread an drift;
An da mey-flooer cleds da burn-broo
An grows ita da clift.
Da kokkilurie covers aa
Laek da white cloods ower da lift ..."*

Hjalta by Vagaland

Throughout each stage of the Shetland summer, the colours of the landscape gradually change as the different flowers bloom. By July, large areas of moorland appear as white as if snow has fallen, when Bog Cotton transforms the landscape. The local name, *Lucky Minnie's oo*, comes from Shetland and Orkney folklore, 'Lucky Minnie' being a witch or troll who gathered the 'oo' or wool from the hills.

Few species are more synonymous with Shetland's upland habitats than Golden Plover, or *plivver*. Their beautiful, mournful whistles can be heard and their slow-motion display flight seen over the full range of moorland habitats. Like most wader chicks, once hatched they spend little more than a day in the nest before they are on the move, picking off a plethora of insects from the vegetation in the watchful company of their parents.

A Mountain Hare with newborn leverets. This species was introduced to Shetland, on the Kergord Estate, from mainland Scotland at the beginning of the 1900s. They were very successful, eventually spreading all across central Mainland. They were also introduced onto Ronas Hill where they were equally prosperous and are now found across virtually all suitable habitats of Shetland Mainland. In contrast the Brown Hare, which was introduced to Shetland in around 1830, didn't cope with the island climate so well and, by the mid-1930s, they had completely died out.

The Dunlin is, perhaps, our most understated breeding wader. More commonly seen elsewhere in Britain during winter in estuarine habitats, the stunning *plivvers page* is a surprisingly beautiful bird in summer plumage, with its ink-black belly and rufous-toned upperparts, not to mention the wonderful croaking aerial song display and sweet trill of the male. They get their Shetland name from their close association with Golden Plover, with whom they share their breeding moorland.

It was on long summer evenings fishing for Brown Trout as bairns that the *peerie haak* first caught my attention. One of the lochs we fished was just a few hundred metres from a favoured deep heather hillside. I knew from my grandfather that the location was where *da peerie haak* nested and so, when first hearing their alarm calls, I would watch from the loch shore. Though distant, their speedy silhouettes soaring and swooping over the hillside had me completely tantalised – I was hooked.

It was thanks to former RSPB Shetland area manager Pete Ellis, who has studied Shetland's Merlin for almost four decades, that many years later I could at last visit nest sites and eventually contribute to their study. But it was from the secrecy of a hide that I learned and appreciated just how special these falcons are. There are so many big attractions to draw us to birds of prey, but it never fails to impress me how they are all so perfectly compacted into one so small.

Merlins are generally rare wherever they are found to breed. Even here, with a breeding population thought to number little more than 30 pairs, Shetland is still the British stronghold for this fabulous falcon. In Old Norse the Merlin was known as *smiryl*. It is clear, through many place names here, such as Smirlees Dale, that they have long been an iconic species in Shetland.

As is typical of all falcons, males are the smaller of the sexes and do most of the hunting. The female, meanwhile, does the majority of incubation and brooding. The male may also take a turn to incubate the eggs, though some females can be quite intolerant of his presence at the nest when chicks are newly hatched.

Only once the chicks are upwards of two weeks old might some females also start to hunt. The prey exchange is easily one of the most exciting spectacles of the season and one that few see, let alone photograph. Returning with prey, the male uses a particular call - an intriguingly submissive series of screeches - to alert the female of his offering. He passes the prey from his talons to his bill, and bows to her as she adeptly snatches it with her talons.

Travelling at almost 30mph, and him perfectly poised, the manoeuvre is the epitome of precision. Most males have preferred vantage points for this, often having different ones for different wind directions which makes capturing the moment all the more difficult.

By the time chicks are three weeks old the parents may make as many as 15 prey visits per day. The majority of prey caught tends to be chicks and fledglings with Skylark, Meadow Pipit, Wheatear being favoured, as well as Dunlin, Golden Plover and Snipe. I've even seen Field Mouse and Wren being brought in. Successful broods of four or five are not uncommon, and are wonderful indicators of how healthy many of Shetland's uplands still are, and why they should remain so.

From hatching, chicks will take approximately 30 days to fledge. The days leading up to their first flights can be very entertaining, with many ungainly attempts made. They will remain with their parents for a further two to four weeks, gradually ranging further from their territory before separating. Siblings often stay together longer, their aerial displays a delight as they practice the skills and agility so crucial to their hunting and their survival.

Common Blue Damselfly was formerly Shetland's only resident damselfly. Curiously, it is very localised, confined to a handful of wet habitats of Shetland's North Mainland and on or two sites in the southwest corner of Yell. Large Red Damselfly have also recently established themselves in a community woodland, where they are thought to have been accidentally introduced as larvae.

Barely two inches tall and with a peculiar opaque, almost fluorescent glow, Bog Orchid – if you can find it – is a wonderful little plant. Breaking convention from the eye-catching colours usually associated with orchids, it may be subtle and diminutive, but it holds its own for its intricate beauty. As a nationally scarce plant, this is an orchid admirers must see in Shetland during late summer. It is rare here, only known at a handful of sites. As the name suggests, it only grows in boggy, sphagnum-rich habitats, and often with Bog Asphodel and Lesser Spearwort as good habitat indicators.

Usually known in Shetland as the *hill moose*, this is in fact the same species of Wood or Long-tailed Field Mouse *Apodemus sylvaticus* found throughout Europe. Given its preferred habitats here, the local name is an apt one, and it tends to be more common on the hills, moorland and pasture land. Three different subspecies are recognised here: *thuleo* on Foula; *fridariensis* on Fair Isle; and *granti* on Yell.

It is likely that the latter is the race found across the rest of Shetland, but it is an intriguing and recognised possibility that other races are yet to be described here. It is interesting that these races, like the local subspecies of Wren, are larger than those found elsewhere, with the largest being found on Fair Isle weighing 32.1 grams. However, the largest known subspecies is that found on the Hebridean island of St Kilda, where *hertensis* is a whopping 42.6 grams. Ours are also known to be warmer in colour, hence they are also sometimes referred to as *red mouse*.

Asides from Brown Rat and House Mouse, these are the only rodents found in Shetland. It is likely that they were brought accidentally by the Vikings. Certainly, genetic studies of our House Mice show that they share the same distinctive haplotype, or genetic signature, as those found in Scandinavia, Faroe and Iceland.

Four hundred species of moth have been recorded in Shetland, and Wood Tiger Moth is certainly one of the more attractive residents. It is scarce but under-recorded here and has a fairly short flight period in late summer and a preference for upland habitats. It is a diurnal flier, with some fascinating adaptations to deter would-be predators – the striking black and white forewing pattern, with contrasting vivid yellow hind wing, is aposematic, meaning they are warningly coloured; and the moths can also secrete distasteful fluids from their body when threatened.

One of six species of bumblebee found in Shetland, the 'Shetland Bumblebee' is the *agricolae* subspecies of the Moss Carder Bee *Bombus muscorum* that is only found here, with the Western Isles subspecies recently having been given its own name. As one of nature's greatest pollinators, bumblebees play a crucial role in the growth and reproduction of not only wild flowers, but also the crops, vegetables and fruits we eat. Better policies, land management, agricultural practices and public awareness across the UK can still turn the worrying overall decline of our flying insects around. With gardens estimated to cover well over a million acres in the UK alone, even the timing of when we mow our own lawn can make a huge difference if we leave wildflowers the chance to bloom.

For a place to feel safe and rest, Otters make good use of dense vegetation growing close to the coast and along waterways. Soft Rush offers this year round, whilst Iris beds are very much a feature of summer and early autumn.

Late summer is peak season for the *herrin hog* in our waters. Named after their association with Herring fisheries and their feeding habits, Minke Whales are the commonest whale seen here. They are generally solitary, however when food is plentiful occasional feeding aggregations can be quite a spectacle.

With their characteristic bill adaptation, colourful plumage variations, and often confiding nature, crossbills are a charismatic species group. They breed surprisingly early in the year in coniferous forests and, by late summer, they are already on the move. Sometimes weeks before we see the very first signs of autumn bird migration, just a hint of south-easterly wind might bring an arrival.

The eye-catching double wing-bars of Two-barred Crossbill perhaps make them the most striking of the species group and, breeding from easternmost Scandinavia across the boreal taiga zone of Siberia, they are the rarest to appear in Britain. All crossbill species' breeding success and movements are highly variable, generally in response to the availability of larch, pine or spruce seeds, and as such they are prone to irruptive movements that bring them west towards us.

In many ways August is an often underrated month. On the moorland many of the breeding waders are still present, while on the cliffs 'gannetries' are in full swing, and during the first half of the month, Puffins are still present in decent numbers. This is the peak time of the year for diversity of cetacean species and, with the right weather conditions, autumn bird migration gets under way.

AUTUMN

By late September, the vibrance and voice of summer has passed. Most of our visiting breeding birds have left, flowers have withered and grasses seeded as the landscape gives way to the softer tones of autumn. However, being the peak time for Otters raising young cubs, the season for Grey Seals to pup, and not to mention the continuing bird migration, this is by no means a time for winding down.

Over 465 species of bird have been recorded in Shetland – the highest total of any county recording area in the British Isles – the vast majority of which have been recorded during the four months of autumn.

From an early-August Sedge Warbler in a lush green iris bed, to a late-September skein of geese, through to a November flock of Fieldfare pausing briefly in a leafless Sycamore, the variety of birds, changing as the season unfolds, offers endless opportunities to enjoy the magic of migration.

Shetland's isolated geographic location provides migrating birds a welcome landfall. At any given period, the islands may potentially host species on the move to and from just about every point on the compass. Weather systems ultimately determine both the diversity and number of species we see here and, for birders with their finger on the pulse, there is no other season in which the synoptic charts, pressure systems, and wind directions are followed and analysed so routinely.

One of the many joys of island birding during autumn is neither the diversity of species, nor the sheer numbers when conditions are at their best, it is simply being able to enjoy birds that we otherwise do not see here, common or rare, which are out of context from their normal environment.

Weighing no more than a 20 pence coin, this tiny Goldcrest will have flown at least 225km to cross the North Sea to reach Shetland and, in this instance, our garden.

*"Bit da hairst wind blaas an da young
eens ir fled,
Da blue simmer sky turns da colour a lead,
An I kroog idda lee end o somebody's waa,
An try no ta tink o da frost an da snaa."*

Naethin Bides – Rhoda Bulter

"Da scroo is erd fastit, weel beltit an snug,
Da dess is richt hung wi a göd net abön,
Da neeps is aa up an da tattie cro full,
So reck doon by dy fiddle an strik up a tön! ..."

Da Hairst Is In – George P. S. Peterson

It's a moment to look forward to each and every autumn, the wonderfully sweet and disyllabic *tsuweet* whistle of a Yellow-browed Warbler. Arriving all the way from Siberia, these Goldcrest-sized warblers have travelled a remarkable distance. The combination of its voice, character and appearance makes this delightful leaf-warbler one of the most iconic birds of the autumn.

Perched on the stems of a *coarn stook*, or stack of oats, this image takes my thoughts back to October 1988. As a young birder of 11 years old, who had not long known how to tell a Chiffchaff from a Willow Warbler, this unfamiliar wing-barred warbler flitting around the coarn stooks of my grandparents' yard blew my mind. Confirming its identification with the help of the RSPB warden, Roger Matthews, I could scarcely believe it had travelled all the way from Siberia and yet, here it was, in a Fetlar farmyard.

Crop fields were once a very common sight throughout Shetland's crofting communities through *da hairst*, or autumn. Traditionally most, if not all crofts (small holdings), had crops of tatties, neeps and oats. In autumn, especially, these small crop fields characterised the landscape of our crofting communities and provided habitat, shelter and food for many species of migrants. They were often even more valued by migrant birds than trees or gardens. These days, such crops are as rare to see as the birds we might aspire to find so they offer as much nostalgia to those who remember their heyday.

Every picture tells a story and, behind this one, lies the discovery of Britain's third ever record of Taiga Flycatcher. Yet it was not this bird's status as a national mega (a birding term for an extremely rare bird) that leaves a lasting memory, but the company in which it was identified. This bird is a timeless tribute to a dear friend who was present at the time, the late Martin Garner.

The weather conditions of autumn in 2016 brought a cast of birds from the far east like no other known before. From late September through to late October a high-pressure system settled across northern Europe, from Shetland all the way into Siberia. These conditions are rare enough but, stranger still, they settled in place to bring us a steady, almost uninterrupted easterly airflow for five weeks.

The conditions were unprecedented and the easterly airflow acted as a conveyor belt for an unparalleled cast of birds including the near-mythical Siberian Accentor – a species never seen in Britain before, or since. For any new species to be recorded in Britain is a milestone event, but on this occasion rather than it being a lone individual, no fewer than 14 different individuals were found, five of which were Shetland. This really did feel like a once-in-a-lifetime event, particularly for the lucky few of us to experience the thrill of discovery.

Snaa ful. Shetland's association with birds from the colder regions of the north is evident in all seasons, but in autumn Snow Buntings are one of the most familiar indicators. This is a bird whose beautiful call overhead is as likely to reveal their presence as their arresting appearance at eye level. It is a relatively common passage migrant in autumn, but occasional larger influxes can occur, though by winter they are much scarcer.

Opposite, Coues's Arctic Redpoll. Hailing from the colder regions of the north, 'Arctic Redpolls' are characterised by their eye-catching frosty white plumage. Hornemann's Arctic Redpoll, from Greenland and north-eastern Canada, and Coues's Arctic Redpoll from the Scandinavian Arctic.

Characterised by their ruby red forecrown, redpolls are a delightful and charismatic group belonging to the finch family. Though they were once considered to consist of several closely related forms, genetically they have been found to be identical and so, scientifically speaking, it has been proposed that they are actually all the same species. Sometimes though, I like to simply enjoy birds as I see them, and put aside the complication of how they are considered in a taxonomist's laboratory.

Redpolls have adapted to cope with extreme temperatures, however 'Arctics' are truly hardcore. With denser, fluffier and longer feathering (which is increased by up to 30 per cent before winter), they have evolved to survive temperature extremes of -50°C, lower than any other songbird. By fluffing up their largely white feathering, trapped air helps keep their body warm, rather like a down 'puffer jacket' does for us.

In order to survive such overnight extremes, in some of their more treeless tundra homelands they are known to roost overnight in little hollowed-out scoops out of dry powdery snow known as 'snow tunnels'. They will also consume more seeds than they can digest while foraging. With an extended oesophageal diverticulum, a pouch in their oesophagus that functions as a crop, they can consume and store surplus seeds and thus are able to derive nutrition outside the hours of daylight.

Snowy Owl was first officially recorded in Britain in 1811 by Laurence Edmondston, although the species is thought to have been known to Shetlanders for some time beforehand. Intriguingly, there are even old but unsubstantiated accounts of suspected breeding here, but it wasn't until Bobby Tulloch's incredible discovery of a breeding pair on Stackaberg, Fetlar in 1967 that these suspicions were first proven.

To British birdwatchers during the 1960s through to the mid-1990s, the Snowy Owl was a species synonymous with Shetland. This enigmatic Arctic owl was a bird that thousands came to Shetland specially to see, following Bobby's monumental discovery of the breeding pair on Stackaberg, Fetlar. The owls bred successfully on the island until 1975 and, to this day, this remains the only confirmed breeding record in the British Isles. The news was huge, and, literally overnight, the island became the centre of national media attention, as did Bobby and the RSPB, who set up around the clock surveillance to monitor and protect the owls.

Fetlar as a community was already accustomed to visiting birdwatchers who came to see the phalaropes, so the island embraced the discovery and the community was actively involved from the outset. My grandfather, Charlie Thomason, was one of many islanders who helped with the building of the observation hide and assisted with the first watches before staff arrived. The owls, the RSPB staff and indeed the thousands of birdwatchers who visited were welcomed, and the Snowy Owls became very much a part of island life.

During the nine years of breeding a total of 23 chicks successfully fledged. Interestingly, in two summers the male was bigamous with a second female, believed to be his daughter, but he only supplied the original female with prey, and so the second nest was never successful. The younger bird eventually succeeded and mated with the male at the main nest site in 1975. By 1976 the resident male had disappeared, but several females remained and throughout the 1980s and early 1990s they were an enduring reminder of one of the most remarkable British breeding bird occurrences of the century.

The owls were very much a talking point in the community. Few summer days passed without visitors to the island, led by Bobby or the RSPB, in search of the owls. Occasionally, I was allowed to tag along. Much too easily distracted, often I'd watch from the Fetlar school classroom window as groups were led through the hill gate, wishing I could go. Sometimes we even saw an owl on a distant fence line or roosting on the hillside opposite the school.

Even more memorable were the many times my father and I would see the owl while working with our sheep in the fields below the iconic breeding site of Stackaberg. It was along these very fence lines, that I remember my father erecting nearly 40 years ago, that I photographed this young male which had been found the previous day just metres from the breeding site. Nostalgic moments like this are priceless. Cultivated by memories, people, places and wildlife encounters, they are the most precious experiences.

With a largely windy, cool and wet climate, it is perhaps little wonder that bats are not common in Shetland. Although recorded annually, only seven species have been identified here, the most common being Nathusius's Pipistrelle. Just 5-6cm long, from nose tip to tail, and with a wingspan of around 20cm, they are one of the smallest bats recorded in Britain. And yet it is a regular migrant from Continental Europe, particularly during September and October, when they are most likely to be recorded in Shetland. Curiously, although Common Pipistrelle breeds in Orkney in very small numbers, that species has only ever been recorded here once.

It is easily the most anticipated time in the Shetland Otter calendar – hearing the short, piercing, high-pitched whistle of infant cubs from the shore. It's a moment loaded with emotion and excitement, particularly knowing we will follow their trials and tribulations for the next 10 months.

Otters can give birth at any time of year but there is a seasonality, driven by prey abundance, so most cubs are born in mid-summer. Only at eight to 10 weeks of age will the cubs first be brought above ground by their mothers. To watch any mother, feathered or furry, caring for and teaching their young at this dependent age is incredible. But with Otters it feels particularly special. For any young carnivore there is much to learn, but for one that must learn to live on land, but hunt in the sea, it's as if they must learn the ways of two worlds.

The cubs' first introductions to Shetland's cool waters is always entertaining. Many appear to show reluctance, even fear of the water, so the mother will carry some of them by the scruff, even under the water, whilst others follow her into the sea without hesitation. At this age, their fluffy, long-haired coats are so buoyant they cannot fully submerge. They will swim on the surface with faces under and bums afloat, watching mum as she dives.

Otters have a short gestation period of just nine weeks, and usually favour birthing places (known as natal holts) that are hidden away from the regularly-used sites, often several hundred metres inland from the coast. While nursing infant cubs underground they are incredibly secretive, even more so than usual, and make only one or two foraging trips each day, leaving their cubs in the safety of the holt.

They are famously attentive and protective mothers and, as the sole parent, they need to be. From those very first moments, she introduces them to the coastal environment and the sea that their lives will revolve around. For the following year, until they separate and the cubs begin to make independent lives of their own, it's all down to the mother to nurture and prepare them for life ahead.

Playfighting among many animals is thought to provide youngsters with the opportunity to practice and develop both social and physical skills. Watching sibling cubs at play, it is easy to relate to this. With their energy, mischievous nature and seeing how often they engage in a playfight, it's tempting to wonder if they play simply because it makes them feel good. Watching them, no matter your frame of mind, you just can't help but feel uplifted. So captivating are moments like these that it feels as if the troubles of the world around you pale into insignificance.

Cubs are usually weaned at about five months, but will stay with their mother until they are at least 10-12 months old. She continues to provision them with prey throughout. On average, an Otter needs to eat approximately one third of its body weight per day so, for a mum of three, she has her work cut out. Although cubs appear to have a close bond with their siblings, to get their share they need to be tenacious. Their determination to claim each fish landed by mum results in some truly spectacular moments. Mirroring their mother's movements when foraging, diving in synchrony, they are instantly aware that she's made a catch and their fight over prey begins before she even reaches the shore.

On a late autumn day of clear skies and light winds from the northeast, there are few sweeter sounds to hear than the trill of a Waxwing overhead. Although usually a scarce migrant, in some years we can see good numbers. They are an irruptive migrant and so, in years where fruiting trees of Scandinavia and Russia yield poor crops, they will move en masse, working their way west in search of berries.

As their name suggests, they actually do have wax in their wing! They have a series of magnificent little red appendages to their secondary feathers which are composed of a waxy secretion called astaxanthin. These are thought to be used as a means of sexual selection – the better the tips, the more attractive the bird will be as a potential partner.

They are famously gregarious and prefer to feed in flocks. In the largest irruption years flocks as large as 1,000 birds have been recorded elsewhere in Britain.

Eating such a volume of fruit means they need to be able to convert sugar to energy, and so they have proportionately larger livers than other birds. While this usually allows them to metabolise ethanol produced by the fruit, they may still become intoxicated.

In addition to their head-turning looks and gregarious nature, Waxwings tend to be wonderfully confiding which can offer some interesting photographic opportunities, especially with some careful planning of where you place your apples, and a full moon!

The opportunity to study or photograph Northern Goshawk at close quarters is rare wherever they occur, so to be here, where they have only been recorded on 16 occasions, was very special. Arriving in November 2019, this young male overwintered in Baltasound, regularly visiting the Sycamore stand at Halligarth next door to our house, where I was able to set up a hide.

Grey Seal pupping season peaks in Shetland during the latter half of autumn. During this time an average of around 1,000 pups are born from an estimated overall population of 3,500 individuals. Most pupping colonies here are on remote and often inaccessible beaches below dramatic coastal cliffs. However, some are on small and low-lying uninhabited isles where they can haul up well out of reach of the sea.

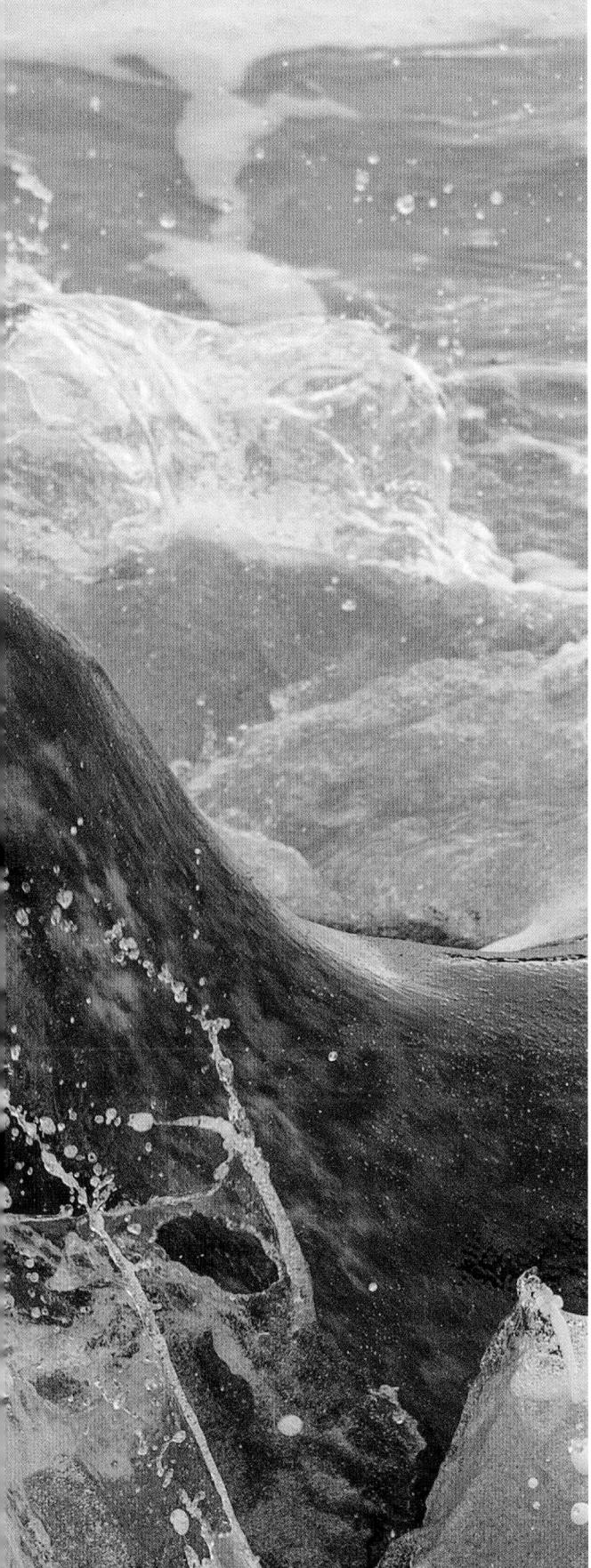

For anyone fortunate to have experienced a colony at this special time of year, the sight, sound and smell will leave a lasting impression. The atmosphere is intense and emotive. Protective mothers nurse dependent white-coated pups, sub-adults practice their social skills, and, there is no shortage of muscle and power – often even violence and bloodshed – on display as testosterone surges through competitive bulls, all hoping to mate.

Typically though, breeding is usually dominated by just a few of the older and more successful bulls who defend small territories, loosely classed as 'harems', within the colony, and mate with multiple females. Bulls can grow up to 2.5m in length and weigh up to 350kg, often 100kg more than the average cow. Cows come into season about the same time as they wean their pups, so in order to maximise their chances of mating with multiple cows, bulls will not leave the colony during the pupping season, and so must live off their fat reserves for as many as five weeks.

Grey Seal cows have an 11.5 month pregnancy. However, in order to give them time to regain weight, condition and moult after weaning their pup, they delay implantation for three and a half months. They are sexually mature between the ages of three and five years old, and may continue to pup for up to 25 years.

Shetland's local population has remained remarkably stable for several decades. Although this is a good thing, curiously it does not mirror steady increases recorded in most of the rest of the species' global range.

With a world population thought to be between 250,000-400,000 animals, Grey Seal is actually one of the rarer seals in the world. Britain is home to over 40 per cent of this total, with the majority being found in Scotland. In Shetland *selkie*, or *roond haed*, were among the names used for both Common and Grey Seals, though fishermen knew the latter as *haaf fish* due to their preference and association with exposed coasts and deeper, offshore waters, known as the haaf in Shetland. The latter's scientific name *Halichoerus grypus* translates approximately as 'hook-nosed sea pig'.

At birth, pups weigh approximately 14kg. They are nursed by their mum for the next 18-20 days, during which time they will gain a remarkable 22kg per day off their mother's milk. At 60 per cent fat content, it is one of the highest calorie milks produced in the natural world. In just three weeks they may weigh up to 50kg, and it is at this age they will shed their beautiful white coat.

Only when their moult is complete are they fully ready for the sea. Before this they are very vulnerable, particularly those at the more exposed colonies where the mortality rate is notoriously high during late autumn gales that can sweep beaches with pounding waves.

WINTER

With less than six hours of daylight and winds regularly reaching storm-, occasionally even hurricane-force, winter is a season of extremes. Dominated by wind and wave, the elements are unforgiving and yet to many an islander, even without the serenity of those rare crisp and calm days, no season shows a truer or more beautiful Shetland.

This is a challenging time for wildlife. The majority of our breeding birds winter in much milder climates, whilst only our most resilient residents remain, joined by a handful of species from the even harsher conditions of the Arctic. Yet though the numbers of species may be fewer, the spectacle can be even greater. Few experiences, for example, can match the sight and sound of hundreds of Long-tailed and Eider Ducks on a calm winter's day.

In fitting winter context, it is from the frozen north that winter hopes are held for an even rarer visitor. That stir of optimism each time you hear alarming Ravens, hoping for glimpse of a Gyrfalcon overhead, scanning a distant hillside for a roosting Snowy Owl or systematic searching of rafts of Eider for a King – the rewards may be fewer and further between but there is an edge to winter birding matched by no other season.

For the species that cannot flee the winter elements, particularly our coastal-foraging Otters that must maximise their foraging time in the short winter days – it is an especially busy time for mothers with families to raise.

"Whin da gales taers da stibble,
An ee belt doon da stooks;
An da lochs is aa cled
Wi flocks o unkan deuks;
Whin he drives da baas afore him,
An der steuch stands i' da sky –
Dan Aald Faider Winter
Is waedin on dis wye!"

Aald Faider Winter –
George P. S. Peterson

White-winged gulls, namely Glaucous and Iceland Gulls, are one of the main highlights of winter birding here and, with a local dialect name of *burgie scorie*, their clean wingtips have long since been noticed amongst our local *maas*.

Amongst the anticipated Arctic arrivals during the winter months is the diminutive Little Auk. Half the size of a Puffin, they really are compact little seabirds. Sightings here are very much governed by wind direction and strength, but when these elements align, good numbers can be recorded during sea watches, particularly during late autumn and early winter. Winter storms often lead to moribund birds being found in the most peculiar inland places and, curiously, they seem more susceptible to this than other members of the auk family. Our dialect name for them is *rotchie* but, unlike most names, it is not thought to have a Scots or Norse influence. Instead, like *maalie* (for Fulmar), it may instead be a name brought home by Shetland sailors during the days of commercial whaling.

Turnstone, aptly named here *ebb picker*, is one of the most widely distributed shorebirds in the world. Alongside Purple Sandpiper, these Arctic tundra breeding waders typify the Shetland shoreline throughout winter months.

With the onomatopoeic local name of *calloo*, this charismatic Arctic sea duck is known here as much for its evocative call as for its beautiful plumage. Long-tailed Duck start to arrive back here during autumn and, by early winter, small flocks can be seen inshore, particularly in the sheltered bays and channels which separate the islands. On Bluemull Sound, flocks numbering in the high hundreds gather on the inshore waters between Unst, Yell and Fetlar, usually associating with the winter Eider rafts, which together form one of the greatest wildlife spectacles of the year, let alone season.

Long-tailed Ducks are the only living member of their genus, *Clangula*. They are unusual in that, unlike other ducks, they have winter and summer plumages, with winter being every bit as eye-catching as summer. As tends to be the case with wildfowl, the drakes are the brighter of the sexes. In winter their plumage is pristine black and white, with a gorgeous pink band on their bill, and a buff wash to their cheeks. They have remarkably long scapular feathers which sweep across their backs and are almost as long as the incredible central two tail feathers, which are an impressive 13-15cm long!

The largest duck in the northern hemisphere, Eiders (*dunters*), are capable of flying at speeds of up to 60mph, and diving down to depths of 20m or more to forage on the seabed. Our local population is thought to be completely sedentary, and more closely related to the Faroese subspecies than their British equivalent. There is, however, known to be at least some seasonal movement within Shetland.

Eiders are particularly renowned for the superior insulating properties of their feathers, famously used in eiderdown duvets and pillows. Unlike goose or other duck downs, eiderdown does not have quills, but instead has tiny, individual microscopic strands, each with Velcro-like hooks that connect and hold them together. The down is often described as more fluff than feather; their Latin name *Someria mollissima* meaning 'very soft wool body'.

Although it is known that Vikings valued this quality, there doesn't appear to be any historic reference in Shetland to this. In Iceland, feathers are still harvested in some places today, but thankfully with the utmost respect of the birds. Feathers are collected only after the birds have left the nests when chicks are hatched. Here in Shetland it was more their eggs, as a food source, that were valued more. Though there will be few Shetlanders now that would know the taste of a *dunter's* egg, my late grandfather, Olie Tait, certainly did, preferring them over those of a hen or a domestic duck!

True to the very northern feel of our winter birdlife, invariably it is arrivals from the High Arctic that offer winter birding inspiration and excitement. Few species or spectacles epitomise this better than picking out the colours of a King Eider, shoulder to shoulder amongst our resident *dunter* rafts in a magical melee of black, white and brown. To the keener eyed, these winter congregations may also harbour other Eider surprises, such as the 'Northern' subspecies *borealis* or even a form yet to be recorded in Britain …

Growing up to 17m in length and weighing as much as 36,000kg, Humpback Whales are huge! Their massive pectoral fins, unique amongst the great whales, are the origin of their genus name, *Megaptera*, meaning 'big wing'. As bairns here we would never have imagined sightings of this exotic, awe-inspiring ocean giant could happen in our waters, and yet sightings have increased steadily in Shetland, particularly over the past 10 years or more.

Humpback Whale populations appear to have increased considerably since the days of the whaling. It is not yet fully understood, however, just what factors are driving the upturn in sightings in our waters. Changes in their feeding distribution and adaptations to their migration routes are the most likely factors, and may represent responses to global warming and changes in the fortunes of the fish upon which they feed. To be able to enjoy Humpback Whales in Shetland is a wonderful thing for their enthralled observers, but it may not be a positive thing. Time, and more research, will tell.

This remarkable rise coincides with the recent increase in sightings elsewhere in British and Irish waters. They can be recorded here in any month of the year, however there does now appear to be a pattern of occurrence between November and February that's becoming more established.

During this period several may be present at any one time and, on several occasions, some have even lingered for weeks on end, offering some truly world-class whale-watching opportunities. These occurrences have also led to some fascinating discoveries, particularly thanks to the collaboration of international organisations such as the Irish Whale and Dolphin Group, North Atlantic Humpback Whale Catalogue, and the North Norwegian Humpback Whale Catalogue.

In December 2016, tail fluke photographs I captured on a calm and crisp winter's day on Colgrave Sound led to a remarkable identification match. This very same whale had been photographed in March the previous winter on the leeward side of Guadeloupe in the Caribbean Sea, some 7,250km away from Shetland. Remarkably, yet another match of this very same whale was made by Lyndsey McNeil in November 2019, when it was photographed in Skjervoy, in northern Norway, by Steve Truluck.

Discoveries such as these highlight just how important the role 'citizen science' plays in furthering our understanding of the natural world, made all the easier by the online presence of the organisations involved, and the connectivity of the modern world.

Proof, if ever it were needed, that not all vagrants to reach Shetland are of the feathered kind – some have fur and flippers. With upwards of 20 documented records, Bearded Seal is easily the commonest of the Arctic seals to have occurred here. Feeding predominantly on molluscs, they locate their prey using their impressive and sensitive vibrissae, or whiskers, foraging in soft, muddy seabeds that, in Shetland, are usually associated with long, sheltered voes and inlets.

To birdwatchers familiar with the frozen north, the Ivory Gull is equally as iconic and synonymous with the Arctic as the Polar Bear. Renowned for scavenging on the bears' ice-flow seal kills, their scientific name, *Pagophila eburnea*, translates to 'ivory-coloured lover of sea ice'. It is a nomadic species that prefers not to venture far from pack ice and so, over recent decades, with global warming and retreating ice, it has become even more rarely encountered here.

With feeding opportunities few and far between, they need to be able to detect the smell of seal blubber over huge distances. It is this ability that undoubtedly contributes to the majority of their discoveries here, as they are typically found feeding on sea mammal carcasses along the coast – a reputation that means that even finding a seal or cetacean carcass in early winter is sufficient to inspire optimism for that very rare chance of an Ivory Gull discovery.

It was with this in mind that I deployed sheep offal as bait on Fetlar's remote northwest coastline and, against all odds, actually succeeded in luring this iconic Arctic vagrant to appear there in December 2007. This was a surreal birding experience and will always remain a fine story to tell, particularly given that, 16 years on, there has not been another bird seen in Shetland.

Whilst winter can hit with weather so fierce it can be frightening, it can also be a time of calm, colour and beauty, when some of the most dramatic skies of the year can be seen whether on the coast, out on the hills or, perhaps even more special still, from home with your family.

Grey Heron is known as *hegri* in Shetland. They are a common sight during winter along the shores of our freshwater lochs and especially, sheltered voe's. With so few trees, it is perhaps little wonder they do not breed, and yet, there is one breeding record, from the cliffs of Fetlar in the late 1800's.

Separated by over 160km of ocean, Shetland's Otters have become genetically isolated from those found elsewhere in the UK. In Shetland they average slightly smaller and have also evolved some interesting behavioural differences to other populations. As primarily diurnal hunters here, Otters prefer to forage during daylight hours. One of the main reasons for this is that the majority of their favourite prey tends to be nocturnal, so resting on the seabed during daylight hours and therefore easier to catch. They mainly locate their prey through their finely-tuned whiskers, known as vibrissae, through which they sense movement of fish while foraging.

"... Bit aa at wance dere comes a stir
Lekk giant turnin in his sleep
Da wind is wokin – rising up –
In peace he can nae langer keep.
Noo aa da peaceful scene is cheenged
Es wind gets fairly in his stride
Lek sompteen driven mad
Da snaa flies swirlin far an wide ..."

Snaa – John T. Hughson

Though we may only experience heavy snowfall once or twice each winter, the conditions can be very challenging, particularly out on the hills for our generally hardy and well-adapted native Shetland sheep.

During these harder times, ever watchful for an opportunity, Ravens, like vultures, are quick to find a carcass and, during these lean months, may even gather in flocks. It's not unusual to see 20-40 birds or more attending a single carcass.

Ravens are known to be amongst the most intelligent creatures, let alone birds, in the world. Scientists have even demonstrated that they are able to complete tasks and puzzles in captivity that not even apes can solve. Amongst many remarkable traits and tricks observed in the wild, they not only cache food for later consumption, but also keep a watchful eye from afar on other Ravens, and will take the opportunity, if it presents itself, to rob another's cache. It has even been known for some enterprising birds to merely pretend to cache food, in an attempt to outsmart the pilferers!

As monogamous breeders the older and wiser adults will stay together in mated pairs year-round. At a carcass they initially keep their distance with regal caution to make sure the coast is clear. Ever desperate to sneak a meal, it is generally the younger, sub-adult birds that make the first move, and feed while they have the chance.

The hierarchy and pecking order in these situations is as fascinating to listen to as it is to watch. Various studies have shown that they can have as many as 30 different distinct vocalisations, ranging from the loud iconic call to all manner of calls, croaks and cronks. In captivity, they have even been known to mimic other birds.

As the more dominant birds move in to feed, the youngsters cower submissively, but inevitably squabbles frequently break out. In the flocks formed of the younger, immature and non-breeding birds, the social complexities become even more fascinating as they establish pecking orders and relationships with one another.

In fact, and contrary to what I see here, in the USA studies have shown that larger flocks of younger and non-breeding birds can actually work together to defend a food source from the usually more dominant adult birds.

"Those who have studied the Raven can well understand how the Sea-kings of the North took him for their emblem in preference to all other creatures. The lordly bird, dwelling aloof in some inaccessible precipice, floating silently on black wings over the heads of more common creatures, dropping with stern, implacable ferocity on his prey, calmly croaking of doom when the sun shines ..."

– Author and folklorist, Jessie M. E. Saxby, 1893

The Raven is a bird that is as appealing for its appearance and demeanour as it is for its intelligence and sheer presence. It is probably due to this that the species has been revered throughout the ages, and has cultural and mythological significance across the globe as a symbol of wisdom, power and even death. With such a strong Norse influence in our heritage here, there is no more relevant example than that of Odin, the god of war and wisdom in Viking folklore. His Ravens, Huginn and Muninn, symbolised thought and memory respectively. In Norse mythology they were said to fly over the earth every day and report back to Odin what they saw. It is little wonder that the Raven is the emblem of our annual Viking fire festival, Up Helly Aa.

By midwinter solstice we see little more than six hours of daylight in a day. But no matter how few hours of light we get, they can offer some of the best light conditions of the year and, combined with even the most common species, there can be some stunning sights.

"...Fir dis is Naetir's fireworks grand
An bates aa rockets ivver seen
Set dere bi da Almighty's hand
Lekk lowin cloods afore wir een

Da very streams wink wi joy
Ta see da Dancers i da lift
It luiks lekk Heevin's haddin foy
Da wey dey mirl an shift."

Pretty Dancers by John T. Hughson

The aurora borealis is one of the most spectacular natural light displays on earth. The process actually begins on the surface of the sun when electrically charged particles called ions are released and form solar winds that continually stream from the sun's surface. When these solar winds come through the earth's magnetic field, they interact with the upper layers of our atmosphere creating heat and gasses which glow and move as 'lines of force' within the earth's magnetic field.

This magnetic field forms a protective layer around the earth's atmosphere which is strongest at the poles and therefore, at a northerly latitude of 60 degrees, we are well placed geographically to see this night-time phenomenon. In Shetland we call them the *mirrie dancers*. Though it is sometimes misunderstood to be 'merry dancers', our name comes from the word '*mirr*', thought to be of Norn origin and meaning shimmer or tremble. When watching them move so wonderfully across the night sky you feel there is no better way to describe them, nor place to enjoy them.

PHOTOGRAPHY

I still consider myself a latecomer to photography. That said, it's 17 years since I first bought a camera. It was meeting Vaila in 2005 that finally opened my eyes and mind to taking my own photographs. I have her to thank for teaching me the basics, and I also owe a great deal to Norfolk nature photographer David Tipling whom I first met some years earlier.

Growing up as a young crofter and nascent naturalist in the 1980s, I barely ever saw a camera let alone used one. Nature photography was a profession of the select few, which made the images created all the more tantalising, and the photographers themselves all the more fascinating. Magazines and books featuring exotic wildlife were always an inspiration, but, more so to me was the work of local photographers. It was the pictures of iconic local species that I knew and loved taken by Dennis Coutts, Andy Gear, and the late Bobby Tulloch, that captivated me the most.

Later I became aware of the work of Scottish nature photographer Laurie Campbell. Laurie focused on the species of his homeland, those to which he felt most connected, and in so doing he utilised his knowledge as a naturalist and understanding of behaviour and fieldcraft. This approach to nature photography was my greatest inspiration and, now more than ever, is my motivation to capture and create.

As a naturalist guide, photo-tour leader, and when working on my own assignments, I feel my biggest responsibility is to wildlife, ensuring we put our subject's wellbeing ahead of the images or experience we want.

For me, learning how to find and stalk Otters as a child, long before I had binoculars let alone a camera, earned me an understanding of how to watch and even get close to the most sensitive subjects without them ever knowing. Trying to outsmart shy species was as much of a thrill as watching them, so, before I even knew what fieldcraft was, I was honing crucial skills.

Nature photography should always be more about understanding your subject, its behavior, and how approachable it may or may not be, than the images you want. The more you know and understand your subject, the better you can tell its story and so the more engaging your work can become. I am a firm believer that those who understand this, before they pick up a camera, make the most responsible and inspiring nature photographers.

Granted, an understanding of your subject or knowing how to approach it may not always be possible. Many species already face tough challenges, and unnecessary pressures from would-be admirers should not be another. It is always, therefore, best to consider the potential sensitivities of the species ahead of the images or experience you want. With preparation and caution, both are achievable with the following basic principles in mind:

- Research your subject – locations, behaviour and particularly guidance from relevant organisations such as NatureScot, Natural Resources Wales or Natural England;

- Be aware of wind direction for scent-sensitive mammals – always approach with wind in your face;

- Try to blend in to your environment – avoid bright clothing, utilise any available cover if in line of sight;

- Keep as quiet and as low a profile as possible – slow movements, cautious footsteps, and try to conceal your silhouette;

- Always maintain spatial awareness – be aware of where your subject might go next, especially avoid blocking route to a nest, set, den or holt;

- Never outstay your welcome – if you feel you have been spotted and your presence upsets your subject, best pull back;

- Be discreet with information on locations – especially for potentially sensitive species.

Equipment and assignments

For some assignments where I share an intimate, and often scarcely seen, insight into the lives of some species, it is important to explain how some images were taken. Firstly, and most importantly, for protected species with 'Schedule 1' classification, particularly for hide work on Merlin and Red-throated Diver, I have been working under a licence permitted by NatureScot for 12 years. Red-necked Phalarope and Whimbrel are also included on this licence.

These assignments, for Merlin especially, take weeks of preparation. The hide is cautiously moved in stages to allow acceptance and, eventually, a responsible shooting position. Only by using the tried and trusted 'walk-in' (and out) method have I ever photographed them. An accompanying person leaves once I am safely and secretly set up within. I use this same technique to work on Ravens. The weeks of preparation, thrill of the 'secrecy' and the intimate insight it allows, is immensely rewarding.

For nest work assignments I have used a remote, motion-censored camera and also a GoPro, however I must state here that such assignments are the result of a great deal of caution, planning and understanding of the species. For Storm Petrels, returning to colonies in the brief window of midsummer twilight, I used a DSLR with infrared conversion and an infrared speedlight flash. I have also used an underwater housing. Aside from a brief few months in 2005 using a Panasonic Lumix bridge camera, I have used Nikon ever since.

THE AUTHOR

Born into a farming life in Fetlar, being with my father on the croft was the only way I wanted to spend my time. Most of my childhood was spent wearing overalls, with collies at my feet, the smell of sheep on my hands, and cows' muck on my wellies. Crofting was my first love, but it had some competition. Even from that early age I was fascinated by wildlife, particularly birds and how they changed with the seasons.

From the Snowy Owl haunting Stackaberg when we took in the sheep, the Red-necked Phalarope spinning on the margins of the loch at Funzie, or the Manx Shearwater gliding in over the calm waters of the Wick of Tresta as we fished for mackerel, the island's rich ornithological heritage fired my interest. In those early years I was also very fortunate to be encouraged by a long list of ornithologists and naturalists which undoubtedly helped set my course. In time this also allowed me to form a more balanced view between crofting and conservation.

It was my fascination with *draatsis* (Otters) that became an even greater passion and would, in time, become my profession. Perhaps it was the absence of similar mammalian predators in Shetland, or how they lived between the two worlds of land and sea, or their shy nature that meant I had to learn their ways, but they captivated me like no other creature, and still do to this day.

I was never one for school or study. On leaving school I did a joinery apprenticeship, and continued in the trade for the following decade before changing course, working on board the inter-island ferries. In 2003, still chasing my dream of a career working in nature, I began to lead wildlife tours. At last, sharing my love of Shetland, our heritage, and especially our wildlife with others, I knew this was the working life I wanted. In 2007 I took a leap of faith and set up the wildlife tour company Shetland Nature.

During this time I have met, worked with, and collaborated with some truly wonderful people since we began, and it is with thanks to the support of an amazing team that we welcome hundreds of visitors from all over the world to Shetland every year. I also work as a freelance ecological surveyor.

I have worked on numerous television productions featuring Shetland's natural heritage, from appearances on presenter-led shows to natural history consultant and guide on the many blue chip wildlife documentaries, particularly those that have profiled Shetland's Otters. In 2016, I realized a lifelong ambition with the publication of our book, *Otters in Shetland – the tale of the draatsi*, co-authored with Richard Shucksmith.

With my wife Vaila, our sons Casey and Corey and daughter Nula, home is in Baltasound, in Unst. Just across our driveway sits Halligarth, the former home of the eminent naturalists from the Edmondston family. The stand of trees they planted attracts many birds during migration, whilst the seabird colonies of Hermaness are only an hour away, the symphony of upland birds can be heard all summer, and I only need lift my binoculars to scan for Otters in the bay below.

For information on our wildlife holidays and photo-tours visit **www.shetlandnature.net**

 @shetland_nature    facebook.com/brydon.thomason    @shetlandnature

AFTERWORD

It has been an honour and a privilege to have written this book and shared these images. The responsibility of celebrating Shetland's wildlife in such a way felt overwhelming, particularly given that there has not been such a book since *Bobby Tulloch's Shetland* back in 1988. In that amazing book, Bobby reflected, with some typically insightful anecdotes, on the changes he saw during his lifetime: from transport links and mains electricity, via the development of agriculture and the fishing industry, to oil and aquaculture.

It is clear that, socially and economically, Shetland would not be the place it is today without these and other industries having grown and prospered in the way they have. From an ecological perspective, the islands might have looked very different without them. But the cumulative effects of these, combined with the evolution of new industries, means that the rate at which the islands are changing is gathering pace.

On a wider scale, the world's leading scientists have highlighted the fundamental issues concerning our environment, and the pressures we have forced upon it, with absolute clarity. Climate change, habitat destruction and biodiversity loss – essentially, the lives we are living are no longer sustainable.

The changes that will make the biggest differences need to be made at the highest level, through government policies and world leaders. But even the smallest changes, made by all of us, can combine to make a massive difference. Thankfully there is now much more awareness of how we, as individuals, families and households, can make better and greener choices – we just need to ensure that we make them.

Even so, reflecting now, as Bobby did before, I cannot help but worry. How will our bairns reflect on the next 35 years? I, for one, hope that they will praise us for the action we took and not judge us for the evidence we ignored.

'Lett be fir lett be', is the Shetland equivalent of 'love and let live'.

Bobby Tulloch